Mr. & Mrs. Greg Jackson

14.95

7 50

THE BEST OF ITALIAN COOKING

THE BEST OF

TALIAN COOKING

Nika Hazelton

WEATHERVANE BOOKS
New York

This 1989 edition is published by Weathervane Books,
distributed by Crown Publishers, Inc.,
225 Park Avenue South, New York, New York 10003,
by arrangement with the author.

Manufactured in the United States of America

Library of Congress Cataloging-in-Publication Data
Hazelton, Nika S.
The best of Italian cooking.
Reprint. Originally published: Cleveland : World
Pub. Co., 1967.
Includes index.
1. Cookery, Italian. I. Title.
TX723.H35 1989   641.5945   88-33872
ISBN 0-517-67949-3
h g f e d c b a

For My Mother
MARIA LEONI

Contents

Introduction

CULINARY ITALY, generally speaking, is divided into two parts: the Northern, or butter, region, and the Southern, or olive oil, region, which meet around Tuscany. Cooking based upon either of two so essentially different fats is bound to be distinctive. To add to the variety, there are some eighteen different geographic regions in Italy, each with an extensive cuisine or specialties and very proud and jealous of them too.

It is therefore extremely annoying to Italians that far too many Americans *will* associate Italian cooking only with an endless web of spaghetti swimming in a sea of tomato sauce, in which a few islands of pizza, lasagne and eggplant parmigiana have been caught. Not that there is anything wrong with these Southern Italian dishes, I hasten to say, but then, how would red-blooded Americans from New England like to hear a foreigner say that all American cooking consists of fried ham, grits, gravy and a dish of black-eyed peas?

This American ignorance about Italian cooking is due to the fact that before the GIs went to Italy, and before travel became as widespread as it is now, few Americans ever came across Italian food except for the Southern variety. Southern Italy is where the vast majority of Italian immigrants to the United States came from, and naturally they brought their own foods with them. Since well-to-do people, especially in Italy, don't emigrate, the Italians who came to America were poor country people, and their food was the heavy, substantial food that country people eat. It so happened that Italian, or rather Southern Italian, peasant food tastes good, and that it appealed to the American taste. It also had the advantage of being cheap and easy to prepare, unlike Chinese food, which is also cheap but trickier.

Now people get about more, and travel and food writers have discovered the infinite variety of Italian food from the Alps to Sicily. Americans are beginning to realize that to Italians the term *Italian food* means very little. For Italians, there is Piedmontese food, with its distinctive boiled dinners and the triumph of the white truffle; Lombard cooking, specializing in veal and wonderful fresh and creamy cheeses; Venetian cooking, based on fresh fish, corn meal and interesting ways of combining rice with other ingredients; and Genovese cooking, with the noble pesto, a sauce made from garlic, basil, cheese, olive oil and pine nuts.

Italians are especially proud of the cooking of Bologna, the culinary capital of Italy. This truly medieval city lies in the heart of the regions that produce the finest and most outstanding butter, cheeses, hams and sausages in the whole of Italy, to mention just a few of the specialties of that part of the country. Bologna is called *la grassa*, the fat, prosperous one, and the term applies to her cooking also. Especially famous are the many ways of preparing ravioli (they are called tortellini in Bologna) in any number of shapes and with even more different kinds of fillings, served with the richest and most delectable of sauces. Tortellini are made by hand, and to see an experienced maker turning them out by the hundreds with a flick of the wrist is unforgettable.

Then there is Florentine cooking, where the olive oil cuisine begins, because Tuscany produces the lightest and most delicate oil in Italy. Farther North, olives won't prosper because of the cold climate, but cows will; hence the use of butter in Northern Italy. Florence also boasts the best beef in Italy, and her cooks have an interesting and subtle approach to herbs.

Farther South, people use not only olive oil in cooking, but also much lard as well as salt pork. Here we come to the robust lamb and kid dishes of Rome and Rome's characteristic way with vegetables, notably broccoli and artichokes. In Naples the food is colorful and displays a triumph of ingenuity, for here much is achieved with little, as with pizza and pasta. Sicilian cooking, to this day, features spices and food combinations that take us back to the days when the Greeks and Arabs were in the area. This is hardly surprising, since the cuisines of the Mediterranean countries are all kith and kin; indeed, the people of that inland sea have been closely entangled with each other for almost as long as history.

Yet, for all these regional differences, Italian cooking is basically simple. The general idea is to present food with the flavor the good Lord gave it originally. Therefore, Italians rely on perfect, incredibly fresh ingredients. To this day, in most Italian households marketing is done daily, and everything is freshly cooked for each meal. Convenience foods are still few, and home refrigeration is not sufficiently common to support a frozen-food industry as in the United States.

The extreme freshness of Italian food is utterly surprising —and delightful—to the foreigner. So is the Italian way of not compromising on the quality of a dish. When the ingredients are not in season (and nobody expects strawberries in January in Italy) or when they are too expensive, the Italian cook does not make do, but cooks something else with what there is on hand. Because Parmesan is expensive, many Italians eat their pasta with clams, vegetables or just oil and garlic, all ways which do not require cheese yet are extremely good. A handful of dough, a few anchovies, tomatoes and a bit of cheese are made into pizza. Small amounts of vegetables are combined into a minestrone. And so we could go on.

Italians also express their talent for making do in their meat cookery. In crowded Italy, land must be put to more profitable use than pasture, and, besides, much of the country is too hot and arid for raising cattle. Therefore, meat is precious, not to be cooked in large, wasteful hunks as in Anglo-Saxon countries, but in thrifty small cuts. A roast, even in today's prosperous Italy, is a festive dish, not daily family fare. Veal prevails over beef, since it is less expensive to slaughter the animals when small than to fatten them. But Italian veal is white, tender and most delicate in flavor, fed as it is on milk only, and so unlike the athletic adolescent beeves that are marketed as veal in the United States.

Lack of pasture and the expense of barn feeding also account for the great use of lamb and kid in Rome and south of Rome. Both animals thrive on the sparse pasture of the thyme-scented mountains of the South.

And of course, Italians eat much fish, since it is, but for the taking, plentiful in the waters that surround the country on three sides.

Italian cooking, of necessity, is quick and done to a large extent in the frying pan. Fuel is, and has always been, scarce since the days of the Romans, and public utility rates are very high compared to American ones. This is also the reason for the absence of much home baking and slow oven cooking. It is much more economical to have a baker bake all the bread for a village than for each villager to bake his own, as in fuel-rich countries.

To compensate, Italians take a great deal of trouble over the preparation of their foods. No American home cook, or very few of them, would spend as much time chopping and mincing away. Some dishes are just too much trouble for an American home cook, even with all of her appliances, and, in the following pages, I have been guided by what is feasible in an average American kitchen. Also, it is impossible to assemble in a book of this size all that is good in Italian cooking. I therefore beg the reader's forgiveness if I have had to omit some dish that is particularly close to his heart.

THE ORIGINS OF ITALIAN FOOD

The origins of Italian food are Greek, Roman and, to a certain extent, Byzantine. The Romans evolved their food, along with other matters, from the traditions of Greece, and they also adopted much that came from the Eastern portion of their empire. We find the Eastern influence in the spiced dishes of Southern Italy, and Roman influences still linger in modern Roman cooking, notably in the use of wine and the taste of sweet-sour. The Romans of old ate their game, meats and fish heavily spiced and even perfumed with musk and amber, and they cooked with fruits, with honey and with wine. Much of this had to be done to disguise flavor taints due to insufficient preservation and to hide the excessive saltiness of preserved food. For salting-down and pickling were the only large-scale ways of preserving food until the nineteenth century and the development of rapid transportation.

Heavy spicing is typical of all the food of history, for the same reasons. Adventurous cooks who've tried to resurrect ancient recipes have found the results inedible. But Roman food was civilized food, and it was swept away, like all Roman civilization, by the barbarian hordes who took over Europe after the fall of the Roman Empire. Until the Renaissance, with its renewed interest in the classical tradition of life that included Roman food, the art of cooking remained buried in the manuscripts of the monasteries. But it came back in full glory at the banquets of the great Italian lords, the Estes, the Sforzas, the Viscontis and Medicis. Their banquets, as painted by the great painters of their time, were worthy of the Roman banquets of old.

The spice trade, too, influenced Italian cooking by adding to it the food notions of the East. According to an eleventh-century scholar, forks were introduced in Venice (which, with Genoa, grew rich on the spice trade) at that time by a Byzantine princess. Their use, though, did not become general until the seventeenth century.

It was the privilege of a Florentine to introduce the art of cooking into France. (Yes, the French historians admit it.) When, in 1533, Catherine de' Medici married the French Dauphin who afterward became Henry II, she brought her own Florentine cooks to her new court. She also introduced new vegetables, such as artichokes and broccoli, and taught the French the art of making ices.

From then on, the French took over. Gastronomy became part of civilized French living, to a degree and an extent never heard of in Italy.

The Italians are very different from the French in their attitude toward food. In the Italian character, there is a fund of common sense and mockery about pomp and circumstance that expresses itself also in the way the Italians look at eating. Food does not evoke deep metaphysical speculations in the Italian breast as it does in the French. Italy has no Brillat-Savarin and very few cookbooks for a country that cooks so well, proving that cooking and cookbooks are not at all the same thing.

There is no haute cuisine in Italy as there is in France, with its galaxy of intricate sauces, complicated garnitures and pièces montées. Not that Italian food is not beautifully cooked and served, as you can see in any good Italian restaurant, but there just isn't that much fuss made over it. Nor do you see in Italy (and Italians love to eat well) the lustful wallowing in food that you can see in France.

Eating, in Italy, is *one* of the pleasures of life. The view is held that there are others, just as interesting and even more rewarding, depending on one's time of life. As Sarah Bernhardt, the French actress, once said: There were two parlor games, and she did not play cards. The Italians do eat, but not all the time.

ITALIAN MEALS

Italian meals are composed differently from our own. They have a beginning, a middle and an end, rather than being one-dish propositions with coffee, as so much American eating is.

Breakfast is either black coffee or coffee with milk. Some people eat a roll or toast with butter and jam, others a brioche and others nothing. Old-fashioned people like a kind of eggnog, consisting of an egg yolk beaten up with sugar until stiff and then diluted with hot coffee. Many people, especially the men, eat their breakfast out, in a "bar," which is a coffee shop with espresso machines, though alcoholic drinks are also served in Italian bars.

Traditionally, Italian families eat the main meal of the day at noon. Working people go home for it, or they eat in the excellent restaurants that the law requires factories to provide in certain instances. Life is changing rapidly in Italy, where the cities are growing so fast that it is becoming increasingly difficult to go home for lunch, just as it is in America. But, by and large, lunch, or *colazione,* is still the big meal of the day for most Italians.

It begins with a minestra. This ambiguous term means soup, generally speaking. But there is also minestra asciutta, that is, dry soup, meaning a dish of rice or spaghetti or noodles. Minestra in brodo means a fluid soup, made with bouillon. The luncheon minestra is an asciutta one, that is, pasta, or rice or the carbohydrate of the meal. Meat and a vegetable or two follow. (Potatoes are not usually served when spaghetti or rice is eaten.) Or else the meat might be accompanied by a salad. Salad is not known in Italy as a course in itself. The meal ends with cheese or cheese eaten with bread, not crackers, and fruit.

The *pranzo*, or dinner, starts either with a real soup, or more formally, with antipasto. Sometimes a cup of bouillon is served along with the antipasto. Even in Italy, formal dinners are not what they used to be, but this is what a family would prepare for an honored guest after the antipasto. Fish, and the Italians are partial to whole fish, would be elegantly dished up under a sauce or a blanket of mayonnaise, with tasteful vegetable decorations. A roast or chicken would follow, accompanied by potatoes and vegetables, called contorno, or literally, alongside (with the main dish). There would be dessert, or il dolce, either a pudding or a cream or a cake. Fruit again would end the meal.

What might be surprising to Americans is that Italians do not make a meal of spaghetti as we do. Pasta is part of a meal, but not the meal itself. The other surprising thing is chicken, the cheapest meat in the United States. Not so in Italy, where chicken is a choice and expensive proposition.

Demitasse coffee is served after every meal, but coffee is never served with the food. Never. Nor is milk, which no Italian above toddling age will drink willingly. There is no surer way of creating a sensation than asking for milk with one's meal in an Italian restaurant in Italy. Nor is tea ever drunk at mealtimes.

Bread is part of the meal also. It comes in the long shapes we associate with Italian bread, but also in rolls. Some of these rolls are enchantingly archaic, being baked in the form of doves, crosses, or cornucopias, depending on their geographic origins. Butter is not served at an Italian meal, except, sometimes, with antipasto.

The *cena*, or supper, is the meal Italian families generally eat at night. It usually consists of some soup, a dish of eggs or an omelet, or a plate of cold cuts, and fruits.

During the day, Italians drink espresso coffee, black, or with milk (then it's called capuccino, or monk, since it is the color of a monk's robe). They drink it constantly, with much sugar. They also drink fruit drinks and, since the war, fruit juices and colas.

In the winter, Italians are partial to ponce, or punch, prepared in the espresso bars by diluting an alcoholic syrup of rum, orange, lemon or what not with hot water from the espresso machine. This drink has been compared to hot hair tonic by people who were not born to it.

HOW ITALIANS SERVE FOOD

Italians are at the same time more casual and more particular about the way they serve food than Americans.

First of all, there is very little eating in the kitchen, and dining rooms are still considered a necessity. They are furnished with great thought and care and, very often, in a startlingly modern manner. (The passion for antiques is just beginning to overcome Italian women.) The traditional way of setting a table is to use a white tablecloth and white napkins, as fine as one's means permit. But lately it has become fashionable to use more fanciful and colorful table linens. Table mats, however, have never really caught on; an Italian lady told me that she considered them unfriendly, dividing the people at the table from each other.

The Italians, generally speaking, have never had the passion for sterling flat silver that the Americans took over from the English. Silver, in an average middle-class household, is far more likely to be a set of elaborately chased coffee and tea pots, trays and other more formal pieces. And when there is sterling flatware, it is kept for company. Nor do the Italians like candlelight for their dining. They like to see what they eat.

But a table is always nicely set for a meal and brightened up with flowers whenever possible. Italian women adore possessions, and china is the kind of possession they prize. This means both family dishes and company dishes.

All food is dished up in serving dishes and never served on individual plates. Italians still have maids, and the maid serves at table. Or, at least, she puts the dishes on the table, and then they are passed around, rather than being served by one person. Meat is carved in the kitchen, and presented on a serving platter, surrounded by neat mounds of vegetables. But the food is never over-decorated by patient hands as in America, since the Italians like it to look natural.

Italians seldom touch food with their hands when they eat it, with the exception of asparagus. Chicken-in-the-rough would appall them. And finger bowls still appear on the family table.

Fruit, in Italy, is eaten with a knife and fork. Apples, pears, oranges—anything with a skin that has to come off before it can be eaten—are speared on a fork and peeled with a knife, and then cut up and consumed like food, rather than fruit. Seeing an Italian peel a banana with a knife and fork, and eat it that way, is quite an astonishing sight.

Italy is still a great country for doilies. It is considered ungenteel to serve even a glass of water as is. It is put on a plate or a tray, on a doily.

RESTAURANT EATING

Italians like to eat out; they consider it festive, rather than necessary. But eating out in Italy has changed during the last few years. In fact, Italy is the most rapidly changing country in Europe, thanks to her new prosperity.

In the old days, Italy was full of trattorie, that is, little inns, and osterie, or wine shops, where good plain food was served by the family owners. They still exist, but far better food is found nowadays in the restaurants. Some are most, and incredibly, luxurious, others simpler. Excellent restaurants are to be found in all Italian cities, and the American traveler will be pleased—and touched—at the pride of the owners and chefs and waiters to serve him as best they can.

And Italian restaurants are not the old-fashioned kind with a wooden stove presided over by an ancient crone. Most often they are equipped with gleaming, ultramodern kitchens and snappy young chefs who are highly competent. Italian restaurants are almost always well lighted, at least those that cater to Italians who like good food. The tables are set with clean white cloths, and there is no nonsense about paper napkins—the napkins are cloth. The average American spaghetti or pizza parlor or Italian restaurant fills the visitor from Italy with dismay and horror, and he turns to the Automat, where the food is at least fresh.

Italian restaurants, however, especially in the tourist cities, cater to one abominable institution, that is, the strolling guitar and mandolin players and violinists. Strangely, many Italians enjoy this kind of hokum too.

When you travel around Italy and want to eat the best of local food, ask the waiter or restaurant owner what he recommends in the way of local specialties. This way, you will be spared tourist food and enjoy the best the place has to offer.

If you want a quick meal, along the lines of a snack, go to a café or bar that features a tavola calda, or hot table. This is the Italian answer to the drugstore sandwich, and it fills a great need for people who want to or must eat out, yet can't take the usual full-course Italian restaurant meal.

The tavola calda is a recent Italian innovation. Hot and

cold sandwiches are dispensed, of a variety and deliciousness that have caused strong men to weep because they could eat no more. To make one's good intentions of eating only a little go overboard even more quickly, the tavola calda is usually flanked by cases of equally irresistible paste, or little cakes, which are another triumph of Italian inventiveness and by far the best cakes ever made anywhere. Paste are small—there are one or two bites to each—and they can best be compared to elegant and diminutive French pastries.

To top off such a light, stand-up meal, the visitor might trifle with one of the sensuous Italian ice creams or with a granita, a fruit- or coffee-flavored water ice crowned with a dab of whipped cream.

ITALIAN WINES

All of Italy is one big vineyard. It has been so since the days of the Romans; many of the wines still drunk were celebrated by Petrarch and other writers before him, including the mighty Caesar.

Everybody with a piece of land in Italy grows grapes. And makes his wine, of course, red and white, dry and sweet, plain and special. To get to know about all the wines of Italy would mean getting to know about all the Italian farmers. Wine is food, wine is as common as the air and it is treated as casually.

There is no wine mystique in Italy as there is in France or Germany. Neither are there great wines in the sense there are great French and German wines. Italian wines are modest, generally speaking, and made much more casually than French or German wines. Therefore, they do not ship or age as well. Vintage years are not usually mentioned. Italian wines are best drunk as they come, at room temperature, since icing destroys much of their bouquet and flavor.

Then, they are a great pleasure indeed. Many Italian

wines can now be bought in the United States, and it is well to remember that Chianti, in the round-bottomed bottles that are encased in handwoven straw containers, is only one of the many Italian wines worth knowing. (See discussion of wines starting on page 16.)

In the old days, Italians drank much wine outside of meal times. This has now changed; wine has been replaced by the excellent light Italian beers. Vermouth and other sweet apéritifs and liqueurs, too, are no longer as popular as they used to be. The Italians who can afford it have taken to whisky and gin because it's smart, American and up-to-date.

Among the fortified wines that deserve to be better known in America is Marsala, both the sweet and dry varieties. Marsala somewhat resembles sherry, and in Italy it is used both for sipping and for cooking. Many typical veal dishes rely on Marsala, and so does the great Italian dessert, zabaglione.

One drink that should be mentioned, if only for the record, is Fernet Branca. Italians consider it the cure to all indigestion and have the same faith in it as our grandmothers had in sulfur and molasses. Fernet Branca is extremely bitter and composed, so the bottle label says, of alcohol by volume 39 per cent, aloes, chinchona bark, gentian, rhubarb, zeodary, calumba, agaric, galangal, bryonia, calamus, angelica, myrrh, camomile and peppermint. Indeed it does cure indigestion. But for any non-Italian, it is an acquired taste, to put it mildly.

Except in super-sophisticated café society—and there is not too much of that, in spite of movies and publicity—to appear drunk in public is frowned upon in Italy. What the Italians think of tipsy and drunk women cannot be stated, because it would not pass the censorship regulations of the U.S. Post Office.

How to Cook with Wine

Italians use wine in cooking, just as they use other ingredients such as butter, onions, herbs, salt and pepper. But they do not pour an indiscriminate amount of wine into a dish as so many American cooks do, under the impression that they are creating a delightful, sophisticated dish.

Too much wine, or wine injudiciously used, will spoil food, the same way that too many herbs or too much of one herb will spoil a dish. Wine, in cooking, loses its alcoholic content, and the taste changes. In fact, the alcohol should evaporate, and a dish cooked with wine must be brought to a boil to allow this to happen. The flavor that is left will then permeate the food.

Wine should not be added to a meat dish before the meat is well browned, or else the meat will absorb too much wine and not taste good. Meat marinated in wine should be dried carefully before cooking.

As for the quality of wine used in cooking, it would be a waste to use a great vintage. But any wine that's not fit to drink is not fit for cooking.

Considering the abuses committed on innocent dishes in the name of wine cookery, it is well to remember that a carefully cooked dish without wine is infinitely preferable to one carelessly cooked with wine. In fact, most of the cooking-with-wine cult that is going on right now is sheer nonsense and has spoiled more good ingredients than one likes to think.

How to Serve Italian Wine and What to Serve It With

It's no more difficult to serve Italian wine than any other drink. The best glass, for Italian as for all wines, is a tulip-shaped one. If you don't have such glasses, serve the wine in the glasses you have. Wine is a drink for pleasure, for the lifting of the spirit, not a cultural potion to be served in rituals as elaborate and unnecessary as a fraternity initiation. But serve it in glasses that are big enough, for wine is made to swallow, not to sip.

An Italian wine rarely needs to "rest" after transportation, the way a great vintage wine does. You can buy and drink it the same day. However, if you should notice traces of sediment in the bottle, let it rest for a few days so that the sediment can settle at the bottom, and decant or pour the wine carefully.

When room temperature is mentioned for a wine, this does not mean an overheated apartment, but a temperature of between 55° and 65° F. In other words, red Italian wine should be served on the cool side, and not warmed up: Nor should white Italian wine be chilled out of all taste. An hour in the refrigerator brings it to the right temperature.

As to which wines to serve with which foods, people should use their common sense and also remember that there is no hard-and-fast rule, especially in Italy. It stands to reason that dry wines should be served before sweet ones, and lighter wines before heavier ones. Italians are very independent about their wine drinking, so why shouldn't you be? Don't listen for one moment to the so-called connoisseurs who'll denounce you for serving red wine with fish. Do as you, your family and your guests please, which is the Italian way of treating wine. However, if you need a guide as to which wines to serve with certain foods, here it is:

> White wine, dry or medium dry, or light red wine with fish and shellfish.
> White wine, dry, or light red wine with poultry and white meats.
> Red wine, light or heavy, with red meat, game and venison.
> Red or dry white wine with cheese, or a medium white wine with cream cheeses.
> A sweet white or red dessert wine with dessert and fruit or, on festive occasions, one of the several Italian sparkling wines like Asti Spumante.

At a formal dinner in Italy you would be served more than one wine. But *in famiglia,* that is, at the family table, all you drink is one kind of *vino da tavola,* or just plain, ordinary drinking wine.

The Best-Known Italian Wines

On the whole, Italian wines take their names from the district in which they are grown, or from the grape they are made with. Among the hundreds of Italian local wines, there are literally dozens and dozens of outstanding ones, interesting and most agreeable to drink, even if few of them reach the summits of the great French or German vintages. The matter of vintage is not significant where Italian wines are concerned, and the Italian growers themselves attach little importance to it. The quality of the wine does vary from year to year, but not nearly so much as in France or Germany.

Most Italian wines are to be drunk young, up to an age of from three to five years. Many are as good as they ever will be after a few months to a year. Only a few red wines like Barolo, Barbaresco, Valtellina, Freisa and Chianti are worth aging.

Basically, Italian wine is drunk locally, and the very best often comes from small, private vineyards whose owners sell to the local restaurants or wine shops. Most of these local wines are not even shipped within the country from one region to another and, almost always, they are sold open—that is, by the liter, half liter or quarter liter. Of course, there is a good deal of bottled wine, such as all the Vini Tipici, the best-known Italian wines, which are government-regulated through an agency called the Istituto Nazionale per l'Esportazione, or Export Institute. By German or French standards, they are very inexpensive: few of them cost more than three or four dollars and most are below this price. Some Italian wines are put into mighty fancy bottles, the kind that make a connoisseur shudder, but interestingly enough, the contents generally belie the bottle and simply mean that the unsophisticated bottler was setting his wares up prettily.

When eating in an Italian restaurant, or stopping at a wine shop, it is best to ask the waiter or owner which wine he recommends. If it is not agreeable, it can be sent back without risking offense.

Of the great number of Italian wines grown, very few are exported, perhaps because, on the whole they do not travel as well as French and German wines. The discussion that follows is of necessity incomplete, but it will give an indication of the great variety of dry and sweet wines, many of which are sparkling. Broadly speaking, the wines of Northern Italy suit our palates better than those of the South, which tend to be very strong and fiery, but this is a matter of personal taste. Also, there are more sweet white wines than red ones; all of them are served with desserts or at the end of a meal. The Italians do not share our prejudice against sweet wines, and right they are too, when the wines are served in their proper place.

DRY RED WINES

From Piedmont: BAROLO, the noblest of Italian wines, BARBERA and GATTINARA, all full-bodied. The bouquet of BARBARESCO and NEBBIOLO reminds one of violets, that of FREISA of raspberries. GRIGNOLINO has a light, nutty flavor. *From Lombardy:* the classic VALTELLINA wines, especially the SASSELLA, and the wines of Lake Garda, especially the ROSSO RIVIERA DI GARDA and the SANGUE DI GIUDA, whose horrid name (Judas' blood) belies its pleasing bouquet and flavor. *From the Alto Adige,* or Italian Tyrol: LAGO DI CALDARO and SANTA MADDALENA. *From the Venice region:* some of Italy's best wines, such as the BARDOLINO and the VALPOLICELLA. *From Friuli and Venezia Giulia,* Italy's most eastern provinces, which border on Yugoslavia: the somewhat flinty REFOSCO and TERRANO DEL CARSO. *From the Emilia:* the famous, somewhat sparkling LAMBRUSCO, with a light bouquet of violets. *From Tuscany:* MONTEPUL-CIANO NOBILE and the wines known as CHIANTI (the true Chianti comes from a very small area near Siena), and prefer-ably the Chiantis shipped in bottles rather than in the straw-covered flagons called fiaschi. The best Chiantis are those from Brolio, Caltibono and Ricasoli. *From the Lazio,* the province in which Rome lies: the wines of the hill towns around Rome, the Castelli Romani, of which the best-known ones are FRAS-CATI, MARINO and VELLETRI. *From the mountainous Abruzzi:* MONTEPULCIANO DI ABRUZZI, reminiscent of wild flowers. *From the Campania,* home of Naples: Naples' typical wine, the slightly sparkling, mulberry-colored GRAGNANO, the wines of Capri and Ischia and the red FALERNO, beloved by Ovid, Virgil, Pliny and Horace. *From Apulia:* CASTEL DEL MONTE and PRIMI-TIVO DI GIOIA, both somewhat flinty. *From Calabria:* SAVUTO, with a brilliant ruby color.

DRY WHITE WINES AND SEMIDRY WHITE WINES

From Piedmont: CORTESE, a truly lovely wine, straw-colored with greenish glints and a refreshing flavor. *From Lombardy:* white FRECCIAROSSA, with a flowery bouquet. *From the Alto Adige,* or Italian Tyrol: BORDOGNA BIANCO, with a slightly sharp flavor, TERLANO and TRAMINER, which resemble the aromatic wines of Austria. *From Venetia:* SOAVE, one of the best Italian wines, the color of amber, with a delicate flavor and bouquet, and VERDISO, an interesting wine with a definite bouquet. *From Liguria:* the aromatic and fine wines from the Cinqueterre, the DOLCEVERE, and the CORONATA wines, which are delicate and refreshing and sometimes tend to sweetness. *From Tus-cany:* ARBIA, UGOLINO and the VERNACCIA DI SAN GIMIGNANO are pleasing, refreshing wines. *From the island of Elba:* the famous

MOSCATO D'ELBA, with plenty of body and rather sweet, and the bright PROCANICO, which is delicious. *From the Marche:* the extremely interesting VERDICCHIO DI JESI, whose characteristics are variable; sometimes it is dry, other times semidry. It comes in distinctive bottles. *From Umbria:* the world-famous ORVIETO, also called EST! EST!! EST!!!,* a golden and transparent wine with a delicate and deliciously tart aftertaste. It comes dry and semidry. *From around Rome,* or *the Lazio:* the white wines of Castelli, especially FRASCATI and ALBANO and the slightly flinty ZAGAROLO. *From the Campania,* home of Naples: the white wines of Capri and Ischia, the FALERNO, known since antiquity, and the LACHRIMAE CHRISTI, both dry and sweet, and, I think, overrated. *From Sicily:* the MAMERTINO, a wine enjoyed by the great Julius Caesar, which sometimes comes sweet, and the wines from Etna.

SWEET WHITE WINES

From Piedmont: the MOSCATO D'ASTI, with a perfume of muscatel, and the liqueur-like, rather perfumed CALUSO PASSITO. *From Venetia:* the sparkling PROSECCO, and from the Friuli the PICCOLIT, at its best when three or four years old. *From Emilia:* both the sweet and the sparkling BIANCO DI SCANDIANO. *From Tuscany:* the light, fruity MOSCATELLO DI MONTALCINO and the VINO SANTO. This wine is made by pressing grapes that have been somewhat dried in the sun. It ferments slowly and takes some three to four years to age properly. Vino Santo is a matter of pride to the farmers who make it, who will serve it ceremoniously as a sign of favor. Vino Santo is also made in most other parts of Italy, but the Tuscan kind is among the best. *From the Lazio:* the dark golden MALVASIA DI GROTTA-

---

* The story is told that a long time ago, a bibulous prelate was on his way to Rome, sampling as he went along. When he met this wine, he is supposed to have said: "Est! Est!! Est!!!," or, in short, "This is it."

FERRATA and the muscatel-scented and flavored MOSCATO DI TERRACINA. *From Apulia:* the MALVASIA DI BRINDISI and the MOSCATO DI SALENTI as well as the MOSCATO DI TRANI. *From Basilicata:* the sparkling MALVASIA DEL VULTURE. *From Calabria:* the exquisite GRECO DI GERACE, which reminds one of orange blossoms. *From Sicily:* some very good MOSCATO wines, such as those DEL NOTO, DI PANTELLERIA, and DELLO ZUCCO, and the excellent MALVASIA DI LIPARI. *From Sardinia:* various MALVASIA and MOSCATO wines and the liqueurish TORBATO PASSITO.

SPARKLING WINES

Many Italian wines, both red and white, sparkle to a greater or lesser extent. Among these ranks first ASTI SPUMANTE, the champagne of Italy, without which no celebration would be complete. For those who like a drier sparkling wine the GRAN SPUMANTE would fill the bill.

APÉRITIFS, LIQUEURS AND MINERAL WATERS

Apéritifs. Italians like a mild drink before their meals, and the very name of it—an opener—means that it is taken to stimulate the appetite rather than knock it cold, as many American cocktails do.

Of course there are Italians who wish and can afford gin, whisky and other American cocktail potables. But they are in the minority; the nation as a whole sticks to the time-honored vermouths, taken straight without ice (traditional), with ice (modern) or with soda water.

Italian vermouth comes white or red, dry or sweet. The one favored over all others is sweet red vermouth.

Vermouths are made with fortified white wines and they are heavily flavored with herbs and spices, in combinations that are the trade secrets of the various brands. Invariably, they contain a smaller or larger amount of bitters and bitter herbs, which give the drink its character and whose flavor is prized by Italians, who like the taste of bitter. The name itself comes from the German word for wormwood. The best and most famous Italian vermouths are made in Turin.

Other well-known cocktail drinks, also in the vermouth line, are PUNTO E MES and CAMPARI, both on the bitter side.

Apart from espresso coffee, lemonade or fresh orange juice, a vermouth, short or long, is what the Italians usually order throughout the day when they go to a café.

Liqueurs. On the whole, Italian liqueurs are flavored with aromatic herbs made palatable by a good deal of sugar; the nation still subscribes to the time-honored tenet that certain herbs are good for one's health, and they may be right at that.

Italian liqueur-making, like that of most of Europe, goes back to the Middle Ages, when the monks were the distillers of the time. Like their more famous French counterparts, such as Benedictine and Chartreuse, many Italian liqueurs have a monastic origin and an archaic, pleasing flavor. A number of them are regional specialties.

Among the best-known liqueurs are the ubiquitous golden STREGA, the CENTERBE (hundred herbs) of the Abruzzi, which is also made from alpine herbs in other mountainous regions, SAMBUCA, an anisette, which is taken sometimes with three whole coffee beans because of the nice combination of the two flavors; this is called con la mosca, that is, with the flies. Anis liqueurs such as MISTRA are found throughout the peninsula, and so are mint-flavored liqueurs. From the mountains of Northern Italy come the juniper-flavored GENEPÌ (GENTIAN), made with the beautiful blue flower, and the KAPRIOL, flavored with bitter herbs.

A part of Italian family life and cooking is MARASCHINO, made from cherries, which, fortunately, has nothing in common with the maraschino cherries we know. The best used to come from Zara, in Yugoslavia. It is still a standard flavoring for desserts, and so is ALCHERMES, a very old traditional potion from Florence, made with cinnamon, carnations, vanilla, coriander, roses, jasmine, orris root and other ingredients, and colored a beautiful carmine with the help of cochineal.

Typical of old-fashioned Italy is the ROSOLIO, a generic name for home-brewed liqueurs in any number of flower and spice flavors, and in beautiful colors as well. I shall always remember the ones made by my grandmother, which came in a luscious purple (violet flavor), golden yellow (mimosa flavor), deep rose (rose flavor) and sand (vanilla), as well as brown, both for coffee and chocolate. I doubt if many Italian women still make them.

Another institution are the punches, called PONCE. These are highly flavored and quite alcoholic extracts, which are diluted with water and, more frequently than not, with hot water. Any espresso café has ponces, and when it is cold there is nothing more warming than a steaming mug of mandarin punch, with water from the espresso machine. For me, this brings back the winter fogs of Milan.

Obviously, Italian liqueurs are very sweet and fragrant. This combines the best of two thoughts: that liqueurs are ladylike and healthy. The average Italian woman will not take to hard liquor and it would not be considered genteel to serve it to her anywhere except in the jet-set circles, which, after all, are certainly not the Italian nation. The health bit comes in with the fact that many Italian liqueurs are sold as digestivi, that is, as helpful to the digestion. FERNET BRANCA (see page 13) ranks foremost among them. CYNAR, a potion made from artichokes, of all things, was extremely popular for the purpose at one time, since artichokes are supposed to be extremely healthful.

Any Italian espresso bar has as a background shelves filled with bottles of gaily colored liqueurs. They are inexpensive, flavorful and harmless, so why not try them all?

Italy's national firewater is very different from her liqueurs. It is a fierce, colorless liquid called GRAPPA, distilled from grapes in varying degrees of smoothness. Grappa is the popular drink, especially in Northern Italy, and you'll see workmen in the early morning down a cup of coffee with a grappa to warm them up. Grappa is not considered a refined drink, but, properly aged, it becomes smooth and pleasant to drink, though no less powerful.

Perfectly acceptable brandies are also made in Italy, though of course they don't compare with the best cognacs. The brandy made by STOCK is the best known, and very worth drinking.

Somewhere between wines and liqueurs is MARSALA, which I have included with the wines. A very well-known Marsala product is vov, made, since 1840, with egg yolks and sugar. Vov is extremely nourishing and is used as a builder-up of invalids. To me, it will always mean sea bathing in the Adriatic when I was a child; before being allowed into the water, I had to drink a little Vov to keep up my strength.

Mineral waters. A great many Italians drink bottled mineral waters with their meals because they consider this healthful. We must remember that spas and their healing waters are an old European tradition, and that one of the most famous ones, MONTECATINI, lies in Italy. Other mineral waters frequently drunk are SAN PELLEGRINO, RECOARO, NOCERA UMBRA, SAN GEMINI, CHIANCIANO, FIUGGI, FERRARELLE, SAN PAOLO and EGERIA. All of these waters are pleasantly bland and slightly fizzy.

SEASONINGS AND FLAVORINGS

Italian food is always flavorful and often piquant and aromatic, but never as hot and spicy as Oriental food. The food of Northern Italy, relying on butter, with rice as its basic starch, is much blander and more delicate; as you go south, olive oil, much lard and salt pork (the Italians use several kinds of salt pork, all much less salty than ours) are used besides olive oil. These basic fats take well to the savory touch of herbs—thyme, mint, rosemary, much basil and sage, oregano—that grow so profusely both wild and in the gardens, filling the air with their sweet, wild scent. As much as possible, these are used fresh. Contrary to what so many Americans think, much Italian food is not garlicky at all, especially in the North. But everywhere, it is the mark of good food not to be obviously garlicky; a great many Italian recipes call for a "remote whiff" of the bud, that is, a quarter to a half a clove. And very often, too, the garlic clove is removed after being cooked for a few minutes at the beginning of a dish.

In the true South, down from Rome, the Arabic influence is still felt in the food. There are far many more combination dishes, macaroni wedded to all kinds of vegetables, fish and meats, and baked with tomato sauce. Here we are in the region of tomato sauce, rich and thick, which is not at all characteristic of the cooking north of Rome, where the tomato is used sparingly. In the South too, we find the Arabic heritage in the spicing of nonsweet dishes with cinnamon, nutmeg and cloves, and the use of almonds, walnuts, pignolia nuts, raisins and currants in nondesserts. But all of Italy is extremely fond of anchovies and capers as cooking ingredients. A very light hand, that is, taking only one anchovy or a few capers, will give an indescribable something to a dish. The same goes for lemon, both the grated rind and the juice, which are also often used for a piquant touch. As for vinegar, it must be remembered that Italian wine vinegar is far milder than our cider vinegar; and so is Italian mustard, compared to ours.

Dried mushrooms—usually boletus, which the French call cepes and the Italians porcini—are also widely used to flavor dishes. They can be bought in this country dried, imported and put up in half-ounce containers. A few, soaked and chopped, will do wonders for a sauce or for a meat dish.

Another basic difference between Italian and our own cooking is the use of consommé as a liquid in most dishes, which imparts a very distinct character to a dish. Where we would use water, Italians use consommé for meats and for cooking vegetables, making them very different from those cooked in water.

Yet another difference that accounts for a characteristic taste is a technique used at the beginning of a dish, in the initial browning of fat and onions, etc. This is called the soffritto or the battuto, by which prosciutto or salt pork is minced almost to a pulp with onion, garlic, parsley and herbs, and cooked for a few minutes, sometimes with butter and oil. The usual Italian tool for this mincing is a mezzaluna, a sharp knife shaped like a crescent moon, and it is most efficient. If I were to speak of a typical Italian kitchen noise, it would be the rhythmic chopping of the battuto heard through the open kitchen windows at cooking time.

One might think that cooking the various initial ingredients as we do, by heating the fat first and then putting in the onion, etc., would give the same results with the same ingredients, but this is not so. The battuto method imparts a savory touch all its own to foods, and it is worth acquiring since all that it calls for is a sharp knife and a chopping board, and the patience to make it all into a quasi-paste.

Finally, there is the use of prosciutto and grated cheese as flavorings in Italian cookery. Italian prosciutto crudo is a lightly smoked ham, and prosciutto cotto boiled ham, the same as ours. Prosciutto crudo, far more flavorful than the boiled ham, is the one that is almost invariably used in cooking, both the lean and the fat, the way we would use bacon, but far more frequently with vegetables and sauces, and for the battuto. It gives foods a savory quality that is more delicate than that of our bacon. Prosciutto crudo is readily available in all Italian groceries; though bacon can be used in its stead, Canadian bacon is a far better substitute.

Grated Parmesan is also used for flavoring dishes, such as stuffings, meat loaves and rice and pasta dishes. Grated Romano, which is more pungent, is used far less frequently, most often in the South, where the people prefer a stronger flavor than in the North.

One last word about parsley. Italian parsley, found in many vegetable markets, is flat-leaved and not nearly as pretty as our curly parsley. But it is infinitely more flavorful and better for cooking.

BREAD AND CHEESE

Both bread and cheese are cornerstones of Italian eating, and both are excellent. As for bread, the Italians prize above all white bread, the finer and the whiter the better. It must also be fresh, and whoever can possibly do so gets his bread fresh from the baker for every meal. Aside from the familiar long or round loaves of Italian bread, there are the panini, hard rolls which too are eaten fresh for breakfast or for snacks. In some Italian regions these rolls have delightful archaic shapes; I remember eating in Ravenna rolls in the shape of doves, crosses and lambs. A specialty of Northern Italy is the grissini, the hard breadsticks made from white flour, which accompany the antipasto; they come in varying degrees of thickness.

Dark whole-wheat bread also exists, in round loaves, but it is much less popular and, in the country, often homemade. White bread, on the other hand, is always made by the baker, and so are the white rolls.

Bread is always served with meals, but without butter. The Italians are so attached to their bread that any government, including Mussolini's, will go to incredible lengths to keep it good and not to ration it without the most desperate need. In the black market during and after the Second World

War, white bread was one of the most sought-after commodities, since the official bread was both dark and damp. A people used to the crispest and freshest of bread suffered greatly in having to swallow such a poor substitute.

Many Italian meals consist of bread and cheese, with perhaps a glass of wine. There are dozens and dozens of Italian cheeses, many of them purely local and not aged. Among the best-known is of course PARMESAN, from Parma and the surrounding region. This, when aged, is the supreme grating cheese. A good Parmesan should be very closely grained and pale yellow in color, with a surface that is combed with pinpoint holes. A good grating Parmesan should be at least two years old, when it is known as vecchio, or old. At three years it is sold under the name of stravecchio, or very old, and at the age of four as stravecchione, or the oldest. The prices go up with the cheese's age. Needless to say, the best way of using Parmesan in cooking is to grate it freshly each time. Parmesan, especially when not so old and so hard, is also an eating cheese, and a delightful one, full of character.

Parmesan is the grating cheese of Northern Italy, and PECORINO the grating cheese of the South. Originally, Pecorino was made from ewe's milk, since cows were nonexistent in Southern Italy. It has a far sharper flavor than Parmesan and is not nearly as highly prized. ROMANO, originally made from a mixture of cow's and goat's milk, is also a sharpish cheese used in cooking, and it is very popular in the United States.

The best-known eating cheeses are the GORGONZOLA, a blue cheese from Northern Italy, which is rich and delicious. It differs from Roquefort, which is made with ewe's milk, in that its milk comes from the cow; furthermore, Roquefort is crumbly and Gorgonzola creamy. MOZZARELLA originally came from the region around Naples and the best was made from buffalo's milk. Some of it still is, and the creamy buffalo-milk variety is far more delicious than the cow-milk kind, which we buy in the United States and which is rather dry by Italian standards. CACIOCAVALLO and PROVOLONE are two cow's milk cheeses that resemble each other in taste and which sharpen with age. Caciocavallo has the shape of an enormous apple, weighing around four or five pounds, and Provolone can be round, pear- or salami-shaped, and can weigh from one pound to well over a hundred pounds. Provolone is made also as a smoked cheese; first it is soaked in brine from one to three days and then hung to drip-dry from twine or ropes that etch the cheese. The smoking is done by wood. Much Provolone is vastly oversalted and oversmoked—a pity.

The best-known mild eating cheeses are the STRACCHINO, which is creamier than the BEL PAESE, and the TALEGGIO. Their goodness depends on their freshness and also on the manufacturer.

RICOTTA was traditionally made from the whey left over from the manufacture of other cheeses. Much of it came from sheep's milk. The original ricotta does not resemble cottage cheese, since it has a smooth, satiny texture, with no solid curds at all. To be good, it must be absolutely fresh, even for cooking or use in desserts.

MASCARPONE is a specialty of Northern Italy, and the best is found in Milan. Mascarpone lies between heavy cream and cream cheese; it is made from fresh cream, pale yellow, and it tastes like the most delicious whipped cream. This cheese spreads well and is eaten on bread; or it may be whipped with sugar and fruits or with liqueurs to make dessert. Unfortunately, it is, to my knowledge, never made in the United States, and it cannot be imported because it won't keep. A great pity, indeed.

A cheese that brings nostalgia to the hearts of Sicilians is INCANESTRATO, a very sharp, white cheese for grating.

NOTE TO THE READER

The recipes in this book have been kept as authentic as possible. This has meant at times following cooking techniques different from the ones American cooks are used to. But none of the recipes is beyond the skill of the average American home cook, for whom this book was written.

All recipes, unless stated otherwise, make four to six servings.

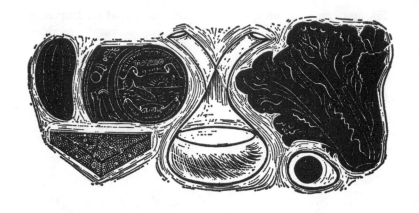

ANTIPASTO,
HORS D'OEUVRE
AND SALADS

THE WORD ANTIPASTO means literally "what comes before the meal" and it should be interpreted that way, inasmuch as the food offered should be interesting and even piquant, and served in small quantities so that it won't spoil the appetite for what follows.

A standard Italian antipasto consists of a little fish, such as tuna, sardines or anchovies, a little meat—salami, ham, bologna or other cold cuts—a few vegetables done up as salads, like beans, lentils and green peppers or artichokes, a few pickles, like pickled mushrooms or the mixture called caponata, hard-cooked eggs with mayonnaise, olives and red radishes. These may be served either singly or in combinations of two or more. When many antipasto foods are presented, as in restaurants, the diner makes his choice from the antipasto cart that is wheeled in front of him. Naturally, there are many variations on the theme, such as sea food, mayonnaise salads or a galantine of meat or fowl; these depend on the imagination of the cook.

What I can stress here are the essentials, as they would be served in a family. These are the antipasti freddi, but there are also antipasti caldi, warm little tidbits that might be made with chicken livers, cheese or ham, on toast or little pastries. But these are not the typical Italian antipasti, which are the cold ones.

For an Italian family dinner, the antipasto will be served from one big platter; it is not usual to make up individual plates, though this may be convenient at times. It is quite essential that the foods be arranged in a very neat and decorative manner, so as to be appetizing. After all, the whole idea of an antipasto is to titillate the appetite for the delights to come.

There is no virtue in preparing all of the antipasto foods in one's own kitchen. On the contrary, no one in Italy would dream of doing this. The Italian salumerie, those combination groceries-delicatessen, are full of the loveliest pickles, galantines shot with pistachio and truffles in highly ornamental patterns, marinated vegetables, olives and other delights. They are expensive, and worth it; whoever can afford them will buy. In this country, gourmet shops bulge with dozens of imported goodies that are eminently suitable, and it would be folly not to make the fullest use of them.

All the foods and salads in this chapter are suited to antipasto use.

Antipasto Combinations

Use a large round or oblong platter, and work from the middle outwards. In the center, place the contents of a can of Italian tuna fish preserved in oil, but drained. Surround it with a ribbon of mayonnaise seasoned with a little lemon juice. The next round might be stuffed egg halves, or egg slices topped with an anchovy fillet and two or three capers, as well as a tiny sprig of parsley. These eggs might be separated from each other by strips of red or green sweet peppers which have been marinated in olive oil. Another circle might hold marinated artichoke hearts, sardines, pickled mushrooms and little mounds of bean salad. The next circle should be meats, such as prosciutto and boiled ham slices rolled up into cornets, alternated with salami slices and a good-quality bologna and other Italian cold cuts. Radishes, olives and parsley sprigs should be tucked between these foods, to give the platter color.

A *meatless antipasto, or antipasto magro,* might consist of overlapping slices of peeled tomatoes and hard-cooked eggs, mushroom salad, tuna fish and anchovies, the whole garnished with mayonnaise and decorated with olives and parsley sprigs.

Bean Salad

(INSALATA DI FAGIOLI)

Place freshly cooked, well-drained beans (kidney, pinto, haricot, etc.) in a salad bowl while they are still warm. Season with salt and pepper to taste. Add olive oil and wine vinegar or lemon juice to taste. Sprinkle with minced onion and parsley; toss. Let stand at room temperature for 1 hour to allow beans to absorb the dressing. Chill until serving time. Drain before serving.

Tuna Fish and Bean Salad
(INSALATA DI TONNO E FAGIOLI)

This is a very popular combination.

Prepare Bean Salad (page 32). For 3 cups of beans, drain a 7-ounce can of tuna fish, preferably the kind packed in olive oil. Cut into bite-size pieces and toss with beans. A minced garlic clove may be added, depending on taste.

Eggplant Salad
(MELANZANE ALLA MARINARA)

1 *large eggplant*	1 *garlic clove, minced*
¼ *cup dry white wine*	1 *teaspoon dried basil*
¼ *cup wine vinegar*	2 *bay leaves*
1 *teaspoon salt*	¾ *cup olive oil*
½ *teaspoon pepper*	½ *cup minced parsley*
1 *small onion, minced*	*Tomato wedges*

Cut unpeeled eggplant into 1-inch cubes. Cook in boiling water to cover 5 to 8 minutes, or until eggplant is soft but retains its shape. Drain thoroughly. Combine wine, vinegar, salt, pepper, onion, garlic clove, basil and bay leaves. Pour over eggplant cubes. (Do not use an aluminum container.)

Toss well. Marinate eggplant overnight or at least 8 hours. At serving time, toss with olive oil and parsley; pour off excess liquid. Serve with tomato wedges.

Cauliflower Salad
(INSALATA DI CAVOLFIORE)

Broccoli Salad
(INSALATA DI BROCCOLI)

Green Bean Salad
(INSALATA DI FAGIOLINI)

Chick-Pea Salad
(INSALATA DI CECI)

These salads are made with cooked vegetables and they are extremely popular in Italy, both as antipasto foods and as salads.

Simply dress the cooked vegetable with standard French dressing or, better still, with a dressing made with lemon juice and olive oil rather than vinegar and olive oil. The lemon will give a fresher taste to the dish. Season to taste with salt and pepper, and sprinkle with chopped parsley. If desired, a litte chopped onion and a very little garlic may be added to the dressing. Serve with tomato wedges.

Note: The flavor trick in all of these salads is to pour the dressing over the vegetables while they are freshly cooked and drained, but still warm. This allows the vegetables to absorb the dressing thoroughly. Excess dressing should be drained off before serving.

Rice Salad

(INSALATA DI RISO)

This salad makes a good luncheon dish when the weather is hot.

1 cup uncooked rice	*⅓ cup chopped green pepper*
6 tablespoons olive oil	*or pimiento*
3 tablespoons white vinegar	*½ cup chopped parsley*
Salt	*1 cup cooked green peas*
Pepper	*1 cup cooked asparagus tips*
½ teaspoon dried tarragon or	*Tomato wedges*
1 tablespoon fresh tarragon	*Green and/or black olives*
¼ cup minced onion	

Cook rice until just tender. Drain. While rice is still hot, toss with olive oil, vinegar, salt and pepper to taste, tarragon and onion. Cool. Add green pepper, parsley, peas and asparagus tips. Chill. At serving time, pile rice on a serving platter in the shape of a pyramid. Decorate with tomato wedges and olives.

Rice Salad with Shrimp. ½ pound cooked, shelled and deveined shrimp may be added to the rice salad, or placed around the rice pyramid.

Rice Salad with Lobster. Add 1 to 2 cups cooked diced lobster to rice salad.

Christmas Fish and Vegetable Salad from Genoa
(IL CAPPON MAGRO)

This is a very old traditional dish that used to be served in the province of Liguria on Christmas Eve, a day of fast in Roman Catholic countries. Few people nowadays bother to make it, because, as a writer put it, "It takes about as much time to assemble as an automobile." I think it is worth keeping this splendid salad alive, since it makes a noble buffet dish or hors d'oeuvre. Make the sauce first, in a blender rather than with the traditional mortar and pestle. The pickled mushrooms may be bought in Italian groceries under the name of funghi sott'olio.

This recipe is an authentic one, but a little simplified in the construction of the salad, which should look like a pyramid. It will make between 12 and 15 servings, depending on the other courses of the meal.

SAUCE

1 small finocchio (fennel)	½ slice crustless white bread
½ cup parsley sprigs without stems	4 pitted green olives, sliced
1 small garlic clove	½ cup wine vinegar or white vinegar
2 tablespoons drained capers	1 cup olive oil
4 anchovy fillets, drained	Salt
2 hard-cooked egg yolks	Pepper

Cut green fingers off finocchio and trim off tough outer leaves. Chop the heart and place in blender. Add parsley, garlic, capers, anchovies, hard-cooked egg yolks, bread, olives, ¼ cup of the vinegar and ½ cup of the olive oil. Blend until smooth. Stir in remaining vinegar and oil. The sauce should be the consistency of thick cream. Season with salt and pepper to taste. Reserve; stir well before using.

SALAD

Do not overcook the vegetables; they should be crisp.

1 small cauliflower, cooked and cut into flowerets
1 cup cooked cut green beans
1 cup cooked sliced celery
1 large cooked carrot, sliced
1 cup cooked sliced potatoes
1 cup cooked sliced oyster plant
Salt
Pepper
6 tablespoons wine vinegar or white vinegar
1½ cup olive oil
2 cups boiled white fish (haddock, cod, etc.), flaked

1 cup cooked lobster
24 small cooked shrimp, shelled
6 cooked artichoke hearts, thickly sliced
6 slices stale firm white bread, free of crusts
Olive oil
Sauce (see above)
1 cup cooked diced beets
12 Italian-style pickled mushrooms, sliced
2 tablespoons drained capers
8 hard-cooked eggs, quartered
2 dozen shucked oysters
24 black pitted olives

In a deep bowl, combine cauliflower, green beans, celery, carrot, potatoes and oyster plant. Season with salt and pepper. Combine vinegar and olive oil. Marinate vegetables in half of the mixture for 4 hours or overnight. Marinate fish, lobster, shrimp and artichoke hearts in remaining oil and vinegar.

ASSEMBLING THE CAPPON MAGRO

This should be done at the last possible moment, so that the various ingredients retain their own fresh flavor.

Place bread slices on large serving platter. Sprinkle with a little olive oil and spread with a little of the sauce. Retrieve shrimps from marinade, drain and reserve. Add beets, pickled mushrooms and capers to marinated vegetables. Pile alternate layers of vegetables and fish on the bread, making a pyramid. Half way up the pyramid, dribble a little sauce over the layers. Pour remaining sauce over pyramid. Arrange the hard-cooked eggs and oysters alternately around the base of the Cappon Magro. Mount the reserved shrimps and the olives on toothpicks. Stick shrimps and olives into the salad, making a decorative pattern.

Fried Mozzarella Sandwiches

(MOZZARELLA IN CAROZZA)

A popular antipasto or spuntino (snack) in Rome and south of it; the name means mozzarella in a carriage.

Trim crusts from stale, firm white bread. Put slices of mozzarella cheese between 2 slices of bread to make a sandwich. Dip into beaten eggs, coating well on all sides. Press sandwiches together. Dip in fine dry bread crumbs and shake off excess crumbs. Fry in about 1 inch of very hot olive oil or lard, turning over once, until golden brown. Serve as is, or cut into pieces.

Note: This is a good luncheon or supper dish, served with a tossed green salad.

Mozzarella and Tomato Appetizer

(ANTIPASTO DI MOZZARELLA E POMIDORI)

Just before serving time, cut thin outer skin from mozzarella. Cut into very thin slices. Cut ripe tomatoes into thin slices. Line a serving dish or individual plates with leaves of Boston lettuce. At serving time, arrange alternate slices of mozzarella and tomato on lettuce. Season with a little salt and pepper. Sprinkle with a little olive oil.

Chicken Livers with Prosciutto
(FEGATINI DI POLLO AL PROSCIUTTO)

This may be served on toast as an appetizer, or as an entree with a vegetable or with mashed potatoes.

1 pound chicken livers	¼ teaspoon sage or more to
3 tablespoons butter	taste
¼ pound prosciutto or Canadi-	Salt
an bacon, diced	Pepper

Trim fat off chicken livers. Cut into halves or, if very large, into quarters. Heat butter in skillet. Add prosciutto, chicken livers and sage. Cook over medium heat, stirring constantly, for about 5 to 10 minutes, or until chicken livers are done. Season with salt and pepper to taste. Serve immediately.

Cold Artichoke Hors d'Oeuvre
(ANTIPASTO DI CARCIOFI ALLE OLIVE)

10 cooked artichoke hearts	2 tablespoons drained capers
(may be canned or frozen)	5 large green or black olives,
½ to ¾ cup mayonnaise	chopped
1 tablespoon lemon juice (or	Leaves of Boston lettuce
more to taste)	

Cut artichoke hearts into thin slices. Combine mayonnaise, lemon juice, capers and olives; mix thoroughly. Arrange artichoke slices on lettuce leaves. Cover with a thin layer of mayonnaise. Makes 4 to 6 servings, depending on the size of the artichokes.

Melons or Figs with Ham
(MELONE O FICHI CON PROSCIUTTO)

The only fruits Italians admit as hors d'oeuvre are melons or fresh figs, served with prosciutto.

½ pound prosciutto, thinly sliced

1 medium-size melon (honey-dew, cantaloupe, Persian or Cranshaw)

Freshly ground black pepper

Peel melon and cut into small wedges (about 2 for each serving). Wrap each wedge in prosciutto. Serve with pepper.

Or use 2 really ripe figs for each serving. Cut figs open diagonally to form 4 petals. Arrange prosciutto slices on the side of the open figs.

Craig's Italian Pickled Vegetables
(VERDURE MARINATE)

A favorite of Craig Claiborne, the distinguished food editor of *The New York Times,* who, unlike most food editors, is an equally distinguished and elegant cook.

¼ cup wine vinegar
¾ cup olive oil
1 tablespoon sugar
1 large clove garlic, mashed
1 teaspoon salt
¼ teaspoon pepper
1 teaspoon paprika
¾ cup pimiento-stuffed or plain green pitted olives
½ cup chopped celery

¾ cup diced cauliflower
1 tablespoon capers
½ cup diced carrots
½ cup diced white turnips
½ cup small white onions
½ cup diced zucchini squash
½ cup diced green pepper
½ cup chopped canned pimiento

Combine vinegar, oil, sugar, garlic, salt, pepper and paprika; blend thoroughly. Add remaining ingredients and toss thoroughly. Chill at least 48 hours. This makes 1 quart and will keep in the refrigerator for at least 1 week.

Mushroom Salad
(INSALATA DI FUNGHI)

One of the simplest and best salads.

French dressing made from oil   *Salt and pepper*
     and lemon juice   *Herbs—such as thyme or basil*
Mushrooms

Have French dressing ready in a bowl. Trim stem ends of firm white mushrooms and slice them very fine. As mushrooms are sliced, drop the pieces immediately into the French dressing to prevent darkening. Season with salt and pepper. Add fresh chopped or dried herbs to taste. Marinate for a few hours in refrigerator. Before serving, drain off excess liquid.

Fennel Salad
(INSALATA DI FINOCCHIO)

An outstanding way of serving fennel as an hors d'oeuvre. Remove tough outer leaves and green tops from fennel. Slice into wafer-thin slices. Cover with olive oil and a sprinkling of lemon juice. Season with salt and pepper to taste. Let stand 1 to 2 hours before serving.

Zucchini Salad

(INSALATA DI ZUCCHINE)

Parboil zucchini squash until just tender. Slice into ½-inch slices. Drain for about 30 minutes. Dress with White Wine Salad Dressing or any other French dressing. Chill and serve sprinkled with chopped parsley. This is a very refreshing salad, but the zucchini, which is watery, must be drained thoroughly.

White Wine Salad Dressing

(SALSA PER INSALATE AL VINO BIANCO)

To my mind, this dressing is far better for cooked vegetable, meat, and sea-food salads than the ordinary French dressing.

¾ cup dry white wine
½ cup olive oil
¼ cup tarragon vinegar
¼ cup onion, chopped fine

½ garlic clove, minced (may be left out or increased to taste)
Salt
Pepper

Combine all ingredients and blend thoroughly. Use while foods to be dressed are still hot.

Parmesan Crisps

(SALATINI AL PARMIGIANO)

½ cup butter
½ cup grated Parmesan cheese
1 cup sifted all-purpose flour

½ teaspoon baking powder
½ teaspoon salt

Cream butter until soft. Add Parmesan cheese. Blend thoroughly. Sift flour with baking powder and salt. Add to butter mixture. Roll out thin on lightly floured board. Cut into rounds about 1 inch in diameter. Place on ungreased baking sheet. Bake in preheated hot (400 to 425° F.) oven for 8 to 10 minutes, or until slightly brown. Serve hot or cold with the following filling:

2 tablespoons butter	*2 tablespoons heavy cream*
¼ cup grated Parmesan cheese	

Cream butter until soft. Beat in Parmesan cheese and cream, and mix until well blended.

Hot Cheese Puffs
(BIGNÈ CALDI AL FORMAGGIO)

A hot antipasto.

1 cup water	*⅓ cup grated Parmesan cheese*
¼ cup butter	*½ teaspoon salt*
1 cup sifted all-purpose flour	*⅛ teaspoon pepper*
3 eggs	*Cheese Filling*

Combine water and butter. Bring to a boil. Remove from heat. Beat in flour all at once. Beat until dough is glossy and clears the sides of the bowl in a ball. Beat in eggs one at a time. Beat in cheese, salt and pepper. Shape with pastry bag or with spoon on ungreased baking sheet. Leave 2 inches of space between puffs to allow for spreading. Bake in preheated hot oven (425° F.) for 15 minutes. Lower heat to moderate (350° F.) and bake for 20 minutes longer. Cut slit into side of each puff and fill with a little Cheese Filling. Before serving, put filled cheese puffs into a hot oven (425° F.) for 2 to 3 minutes, to heat them through. Serve very hot.

CHEESE FILLING

¼ cup butter
½ cup flour
½ teaspoon salt
¼ teaspoon pepper

¾ cup milk
½ cup grated Parmesan cheese
1 egg yolk

Melt butter. Remove from heat. Stir in flour and seasonings. Gradually stir in milk, stirring until well blended and smooth. Cook over low heat, stirring constantly, until very thick and smooth. Beat in cheese and egg yolk. Cook until the mixture is blended and the cheese melted. Makes about 1¼ cup of sauce.

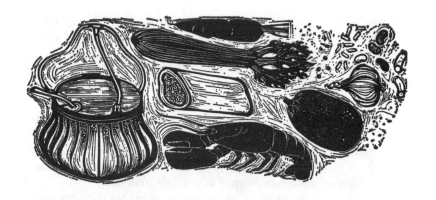

SOUPS

ITALIANS ARE GREAT SOUP EATERS. Soup starts a meal, and soup, especially in the evening, is the meal. There are thick peasant soups of vegetables and rice, pasta and other starches to appease the hunger of hard-working, out-of-doors people and thin, concentrated consommés to titillate the appetite at a pranzo, an elegant dinner party.

There are three basic kinds of soup. First, those made with or consisting of il brodo—consommé or broth made from meat, chicken, fish or vegetables; they are called minestre in brodo. A brodo may be served plain, or it may contain eggs, rice, a small pasta, bits of meat, a dumpling or tiny ravioli or a vegetable. Then there are the combinations of one or several fresh and dried vegetables, whatever is at hand, sometimes again with pasta or rice or meat. These are on the thick side, and often called minestrone, that is, a big soup.

Finally, there are the cream soups, which resemble French cream soups and which are not quite as typical of Italian cooking as the first two.

What characterizes all Italian soups, whether thick or thin (with the exception of some cream soups), is the generous use of grated Parmesan or Romano cheese. The cheese is served separately at the table, and each diner helps himself to taste. With the exception of il brodo in tazza, a concentrated consommé served in cups at elegant dinner parties, Italian soups are eaten from large soup plates, so that cheese and soup ingredients can be stirred into a delicious whole.

Another characteristic of Italian soups is that they are very often a product of whatever ingredients are at hand. The vegetable soups especially depend on the season and the availability of ingredients, and any Italian cook will know how to produce a soup from what there is in the house. The final taste will have a regional character, since all Italian food is so heavily regional. To give a few examples, in Milan, the cook will use rice rather than pasta to thicken her soup, and in Southern Italy it will be the other way around. In Tuscany, olive oil and beans will be popular; in Rome, lard and chick peas may take their place. And as in all Italian cooking, the soups of the North will be lighter and more delicate than those of the South. Three more things should be borne in mind. First, the prevalent use of brodo or consommé as the soup liquid. It may be beef, chicken or vegetable, but, whatever, it gives a soup a far more substantial and flavorful quality than water. Homemade consommé or a good quality canned consommé are far the best to use, but in many thick, rich soups consommé made with a bouillon cube or dehydrated bouillon powder will be adequate. Second, soup, unless it is clear consommé, is never served at the same meal as a pasta or rice dish; one eats either one or the other. Finally, the word minestra means more than its literal English translation, soup. It also means the first course of a meal, after the antipasto or hors d'oeuvre. Rice and pasta dishes are therefore also called minestra or minestre, to use the word's plural. Thus we have a minestra in brodo, that is, a liquid, or real, soup and a minestra asciutta, a dry soup, which can be a risotto, spaghetti or any other such dish.

Consommé

(IL BRODO)

This is the cornerstone of Italian cookery, since it is used not only for soups, but also in all sorts of dishes instead of water. Clear beef consommé is the most commonly used brodo, and it is liked good and strong. Veal consommé is made from veal and veal bones, mostly for invalid feeding; it is less appreciated because it is not quite as tasty as beef consommé. Chicken consommé is not as frequently used as in the United States. Formerly, brodo was always made at home and it was the test of a cook; nowadays, bouillon cubes and bouillon powders are extremely popular. Italian bouillon cubes are more concentrated and more highly seasoned than ours.

3 pounds best soup meat, such as shin	*1 stalk celery, chopped*
	1 medium onion, chopped
3 pounds beef bones, including marrow bones	*3 sprigs parsley*
	3 quarts cold water
1 large carrot, chopped	

Combine all ingredients in a large kettle. Bring to a boil. Boil over medium heat for 5 to 10 minutes. With a large spoon or ladle, skim off any scum that has come to the surface. Reduce heat to lowest possible. Simmer, covered, for 2½ hours. Strain soup through several layers of cheesecloth or a clean kitchen towel. Cool, uncovered. Chill and remove fat layer on top before using.

Consommé with Egg
(STRACCIATELLA)

This famous soup comes from Rome—but it turns up under different names in other parts of Italy. The word means the ragged one. Delicate, nourishing and quickly made, it is used to introduce both family and party meals, and for invalid food.

3 *eggs*
3 *tablespoons farina or Cream of Wheat*
3 *tablespoons grated Parmesan cheese*
1 *cup cold clear beef or chicken bouillon*

8 *cups clear beef or chicken bouillon, at boiling point*
Salt
Pepper

In a bowl, beat together eggs, farina and Parmesan cheese. Gradually stir in the cold bouillon and beat until smooth. Over low heat, stir mixture into boiling bouillon, beating with a wire whisk or a fork to obtain a flaky texture. Simmer, stirring constantly, for about 5 minutes. If necessary, season with salt and pepper, but the bouillon and cheese may be seasoning enough for this soup. Serve with additional grated Parmesan cheese.

Consommé Mille Fanti
(MINESTRA MILLE FANTI)

This is the Northern Italian version of the Roman stracciatella and an equally famous soup. The name means a thousand lads and refers to the shredded filling of the soup. The difference between the two soups is that Mille Fanti uses fresh bread crumbs instead of farina, and a touch of nutmeg for seasoning. The recipes advocating flour are not correct, since flour would give a somewhat sticky quality to the soup. The bread crumbs should be very fine; they can be made so by pushing fresh white bread crumbs through a strainer.

3 *eggs*	*⅛ teaspoon nutmeg*
¼ cup fresh white bread crumbs	*6 to 8 cups clear beef or chicken consommé, at boiling point*
3 tablespoons grated Parmesan cheese	*Salt*
	Pepper

In a bowl, beat eggs. Beat in bread crumbs, Parmesan cheese and nutmeg, beating until smooth. Add salt and pepper to taste. With wire whisk or fork, stir mixture into boiling consommé. Simmer, covered, over lowest possible heat for 5 to 7 minutes. Stir thoroughly before serving with additional Parmesan cheese.

Annetta Anghileri's Soup

(LA MINESTRA DI ANNETTA ANGHILERI)

An excellent light soup and an example of how Italians can make a few simple ingredients go a very long way.

6 to 8 cups beef or chicken consommé	*1 cup chopped parsley*
2 tablespoons butter	*¼ pound sliced mushrooms*
⅓ cup uncooked rice	*½ cup shelled or frozen peas*

Bring consommé to a boil. Add butter; lower heat to lowest possible. Add rice, parsley, mushrooms and peas. Simmer, covered, for 45 minutes to 1 hour.

Note: This soup may also be cooked just until the rice is done. But the original long cooking time produces a delicious blend of flavors.

Thick Pasta and Bean Soup
(MINESTRA DI PASTA E FAGIOLI)

This soup is called Pasta e Fazul in Southern Italy, but it is eaten anywhere from Florence down. Made with fresh beans, which can be bought seasonally in Italian vegetable markets, it is even better. This soup can be made as thick or as thin as one likes, like all the popular Italian soups. Simply increase or decrease the bouillon.

½ pound dried pinto, navy or other beans
1 quart water
1 cup tomato sauce
4 to 6 cups hot bouillon or water
2 tablespoons lard
½ cup chopped salt pork or bacon

1 medium onion, minced
1 garlic clove, minced
1 tablespoon flour
Salt
¼ teaspoon crushed red pepper or pepper to taste
½ pound ditalini or other small pasta
½ cup chopped parsley

Soak beans in water overnight, or pour boiling water over beans and let stand for 1 hour. Cook beans in the same water until half tender. Add tomato sauce and bouillon. While beans are cooking, heat together the lard, salt pork, onion and garlic. Cook, stirring constantly, until onion is soft. Stir in flour and about 1 cup of the bean liquid. Add to beans. Season with salt and pepper. Simmer, covered, until beans are almost done. Add ditalini and cook until tender. Sprinkle with parsley and serve with plenty of grated Parmesan or Romano cheese.

Tripe Soup from Milan

(LA BUSECCA)

A very traditional dish, which is a thick vegetable soup with veal tripe added to it. Buy partially precooked tripe for this dish. Tripe must be cooked over very low heat, or it gets tough when it should be soft.

3 pounds partially precooked tripe	½ small cabbage, shredded
Boiling water	4 medium tomatoes, peeled, seeded and chopped or 2 tablespoons tomato sauce
2 small onions	
4 whole cloves	Salt
2 stalks celery	Pepper
4 slices bacon, minced	1 cup cooked navy or pinto beans
3 tablespoons butter	
2 carrots, diced	Toasted slices of Italian bread
4 medium potatoes, diced	Grated Parmesan cheese

Wash tripe and cut into narrow strips. Put into deep kettle. Add boiling water to cover, one of the onions stuck with the cloves and one of the celery stalks. Simmer, covered, over lowest possible heat until almost tender. (Cooking time varies with the kind of tripe and the length of time it was precooked.) Mince remaining onion and celery stalk. In another deep kettle, heat together minced bacon and butter. Add minced onion and celery. Cook over medium heat, stirring constantly, until onion is soft. Add carrots, potatoes, cabbage, tomatoes and salt and pepper to taste. Cook, stirring constantly, for 2 minutes. Remove whole onion and celery stalk from cooked tripe. Add tripe and the liquid in which it was cooked to vegetable mixture. Simmer, covered, over lowest possible heat for about 45 minutes or until tripe and vegetables are tender. Add beans and cook 10 minutes longer. If the soup is too thick, add a little more hot water to achieve a desired consistency. Serve over toasted slices of Italian bread with plenty of grated Parmesan cheese.

Italian Fish Soup
(ZUPPA DI PESCE)

There are as many fish soups as there are Mediterranean countries, and they are generally made with whatever fish is handy. They do not differ from each other very much. Since our American fish are different, I give a modified version of the famous zuppa di pesce from the Danieli in Venice. The luxurious Danieli, on the Riva degli Schiavoni, is one of the world's most romantic hotels, with a melting view of the city and lagoon.

1½ pounds lobster, cut up	2 garlic cloves, minced
½ pound shrimp	2 bay leaves, crumbled
1 quart water	½ teaspoon thyme
1 onion, sliced	1 teaspoon basil
1 stalk celery with leaves, sliced	2 tablespoons chopped parsley
	4 cups fish broth
2 tablespoons vinegar	½ cup dry white wine
2 tablespoons salt	1½ cups chopped peeled tomatoes
2½ pounds mixed whole fish, such as haddock, trout, cod, red snapper	Pinch of saffron (optional)
	Salt
¼ cup oil	Pepper

Boil lobster and shrimp for 5 minutes in water with onion, celery, vinegar and salt. Remove, reserve broth, and shell lobster and shrimp. Save shells. Cut heads and tails off fish and, with lobster and shrimp shells, add to broth. Simmer for 20 minutes. Strain, and set broth aside. Cut up lobster and fish into bite-size chunks and cut shrimps in half. Heat oil, and sauté fish with garlic, bay leaves, thyme, basil and parsley for 5 minutes, stirring constantly. Add fish broth, wine, tomatoes, saffron, salt and pepper. Bring to a quick boil, cover and simmer for 20 minutes. Serves 8 to 10. Serve with slices of bread or polenta fried in oil.

Note: To make this soup more authentic, ½ pound squid may be added and cooked with the lobster and shrimp.

Spinach and Rice Soup

(ZUPPA DI RISO E SPINACI)

An Italian classic that does not depend on strictly measured ingredients. It is just rice and spinach cooked together in broth to the desired consistency.

1 pound fresh or 1 to 2 10-
    ounce packages frozen,
    spinach
8 cups beef or chicken bouil-
    lon

½ cup uncooked rice
Salt
Pepper
⅛ teaspoon nutmeg (optional)
Freshly grated Parmesan cheese

With kitchen scissors cut coarse stems off spinach and cut leaves into shreds. Bring bouillon to boil. Add rice. Simmer, covered, until rice is almost cooked. Add spinach. Season with salt, pepper and nutmeg. Cook 3 minutes longer; the spinach should be still firm. Serve with grated Parmesan cheese.

Milanese Rice and Cabbage Soup

(RISO E VERZA ALLA MILANESE)

Have a thicker or thinner soup by decreasing or increasing the quantity of consommé.

1 tablespoon lard
2 tablespoons minced parsley
1 small cabbage or Savoy cab-
    bage
Boiling water
8 to 9 cups boiling consommé

1 garlic clove
1 cup uncooked rice
Salt
Pepper
Grated Parmesan cheese

Cream together lard and parsley. Remove tough outer leaves from cabbage. Trim off coarse stalks. Chop coarsely. Cook in boiling water to cover for 3 minutes. Drain. Put cabbage into deep kettle. Add 1 cup of the boiling consommé, garlic and the lard and parsley mixture. Simmer, covered, over lowest possible heat for 15 minutes. Remove garlic clove. Add remaining boiling consommé and rice. Season with salt and pepper to taste. Cook, uncovered, over medium heat until rice is tender. Serve with grated Parmesan cheese.

Minestrone from Milan

(MINESTRONE ALLA MILANESE)

One of the many versions of Italy's most famous soup. Contrary to a common American belief, a minestrone is not a catch-all of every available vegetable, but a mixture of judiciously balanced ones. What makes this soup typical of Milan is the use of rice where minestroni from other cities might use some kind of pasta.

2 tablespoons butter
2 tablespoons minced
    blanched salt pork
½ medium onion, minced
1 garlic clove
1 veal shank bone
3 tomatoes, peeled and
    chopped
4 medium potatoes, peeled
1 cup shelled fresh kidney or
    other beans
1 sliced leek, white and green
    parts
2 celery stalks, sliced
1 carrot, cubed

¼ cup minced parsley
½ teaspoon ground sage or 4
    leaves dried sage, crumbled
¼ teaspoon dried rosemary,
    crumbled
¼ teaspoon ground oregano
¼ teaspoon dried basil
2 cups hot consommé
2½ quarts boiling water
1 cup beet greens, shredded
2 cups shelled peas
1 cup uncooked rice
2 tablespoons butter
½ cup grated Parmesan cheese
1 tablespoon minced parsley

In a deep kettle, cook together butter, salt pork, onion and the garlic clove until onion is soft. Remove garlic clove and throw away. Add veal shank bone and tomatoes. Cook over medium heat for 3 minutes or until bone is golden on all sides. Cut 2 of the potatoes into small dice. Add diced potatoes, beans, leek, celery and carrot to kettle. Combine parsley, sage, rosemary, oregano and basil. Divide into 2 parts. Add 1 part to vegetables. Simmer over lowest possible heat, stirring constantly, for 5 minutes. Add consommé and the 2 whole potatoes. Simmer, covered, stirring occasionally, for 15 minutes. Add boiling water. Simmer, covered, for 1½ hours. Mash whole potatoes with a fork against the sides of the kettle. Add remaining parsley and herb mixture, beet greens and peas. When the soup has started to boil again, add rice. Cook over medium heat, stirring occasionally, until rice is tender. Remove veal shank bone. Cream together butter, Parmesan and parsley. Remove soup from heat. Stir butter mixture into soup before serving. Serve with additional grated Parmesan cheese.

Note: This Minestrone is eaten cooled, but not chilled, during the hot season. It is excellent.

Pasta and Chick-Pea Soup
(MINESTRA DI PASTA E CECI)

This is a Roman specialty, somewhere between a soup and a stew. It is heavy and utterly delicious. The recipe makes 3 quarts, about enough to feed 8 to 10 hungry people. I make pasta e ceci for picnics, taking it along in an insulated bag, since it does not have to be eaten absolutely hot. With some ripe tomatoes to be eaten out of hand, wine, bread and cheese, and a slab of bitter chocolate for dessert, the pasta e ceci makes most successful picnic food.

¾ cup olive oil
3 large cloves garlic, minced
8 anchovy fillets, minced
1 cup chopped parsley
2 1-pound cans chick peas
   (about 4⅔ cups)
4 large tomatoes, peeled,
   seeded and chopped

1 tablespoon dried rosemary
1 quart water
1 pound ditalini #48 or elbow
   macaroni
2 tablespoons salt
4 to 6 quarts rapidly boiling
   water
Grated Parmesan or Romano
   cheese

In large kettle, heat oil and cook garlic, anchovies and parsley in it over low heat for 5 minutes. Add undrained chick peas, tomatoes, rosemary, and 1 quart water. Cover and cook over low heat 30 minutes, stirring frequently. Cook ditalini or elbow macaroni in boiling water to which 2 tablespoons salt have been added. Cook uncovered, stirring occasionally, about 8 minutes, or until not quite, but almost, tender. Drain.

Add ditalini or elbow macaroni to soup. Cook another 5 minutes, or until ditalini is tender. Stir occasionally, and serve with plenty of grated cheese.

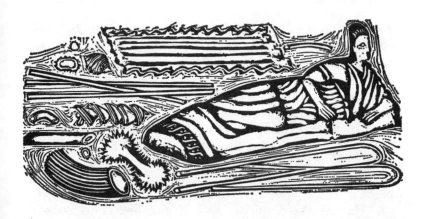

SPAGHETTI, MACARONI
AND OTHER PASTA

Amorini (little cupids), cappelli di prete (priests' hats), creste di gallo (coxcombs), mille righe (a thousand stripes), ricciolini (little curls), stivaletti (little boots), lingue di passero (sparrows' tongues), lumache, lumachine and lumacone (snails, little snails and big snails), mostaccioli (little moustaches), occhi di lupo (wolf's eyes), vermicelli (little worms) are but a few of the hundred-odd names given to the various offspring of the pasta family, according to the learned Dr. Mario Pei, who teaches Romance philology at Columbia University in New York.

The very folkloristic sound of these names shows the close union between the Italian and his macaroni. Though there is a misty legend that Marco Polo brought macaroni back from China, where it had been known for thousands of years (this is no legend), macaroni was well known in Italy before Marco Polo's day. In the year 1200, a document called the *Life of the Blessed Hermit William* mentioned: "He invited William to dinner and served macaroni!" Indeed, pasta may well have been known much earlier in the Mediterranean: lasagne, the broad noodles, is a word that comes from the Greek and the Latin. Among the exhibits in the museum at Pompeii there is equipment used by the ancients to make, cook and serve pasta.

Through the centuries, we find macaroni and literature linked together. Boccaccio, in the *Decameron*, describes an idyllic country where no one works and all things are free, with a mountain of grated cheese in the middle of it. On top of this mountain, there are people who do nothing but make pasta, which they cook in capon broth, and then dispense to all who want it. The eighteenth-century playwright Goldoni tells how he tossed down three platefuls of macaroni, and described it as a marvelous moment. Or, as the Neapolitan proverb has it, "He fell into it, like macaroni into the cheese," not a surprising thing since, during the seventeenth century, Naples established itself as the macaroni capital of Italy.

Pasta, literally translated as paste, is the basic food of middle and Southern Italy, and there are countless ways of serving it, both rich and plain ones. The Italian nation was happy with its favorite food until the thirties, when the Futurist poet Marinetti started lashing out against all established cookery, and especially against pasta asciutta, that is, a pasta dish not cooked in broth. He declared it an obsolete food, to use one of the milder statements of this poet, who specialized in a language that was as florid as it was vehement. Another statement of his was that macaroni induces skepticism and pessimism. He might have been right about this; the Italians are, as a nation, both skeptical and pessimistic.

Marinetti's statements created a great commotion even among people who usually ignore these things. This time they got into the strife, and the Duke of Bovino, then mayor of Naples, said, "The angels in Paradise eat nothing but Vermicelli al Pomodoro," that is, with tomato sauce. Marinetti replied that this confirmed his worst suspicions about the monotony of paradise and the kind of life led by the angels.

Nor did Marinetti wean the Italians from their favorite food; they lead in pasta consumption, with the Swiss coming in a poor second.

If anyone wonders how macaroni got into "Yankee Doodle," the story is this: In eighteenth-century London, the café society of the time congregated in "Macaroni Clubs." *Scots Magazine* for November 1772 says: "Macaroni was far from being universally known in this country until the commencement of the last peace when, like many other foreign fashions, it was imported by our cognoscenti in eating, as an improvement to the subscription table at Almack's [a club]. In time, the subscribers to these dinners came to be distinguished by the title of 'macaroni' and as the meeting was composed of the younger and gayer part of our nobility and gentry, who, at the same time that they gave into our luxuries of eating, went equally into the extravagancy of dress, the word 'macaroni' changed its meaning to that of a person who exceeded the ordinary bounds of fashion, and is justly used as a term of reproach of all kinds of people, indifferently, who fall into absurdity."

The word *macaroni* crossed the Atlantic at this time, and toward the end of the 1700s Americans were singing about macaroni without knowing what it was all about. It is said that "stuck a feather in his cap and called it macaroni" meant that Yankee Doodle was a dude at the time the word macaroni stood for dandyism, and that the poet used the word, which rhymes with pony, to express the elegant touch.

No less a man than Thomas Jefferson introduced macaroni

into America. Along with Lombardy poplars, Palladian architecture, Tuscan wine, French home furnishings and countless gourmet recipes gathered when he was Ambassador to France, the Master of Monticello imported the first spaghetti-making machine into America. His macaroni recipes, however, are rather uninteresting.

Only too few ways of eating pasta are known in America, even today. Tomato sauce and meatballs are just the beginning. All pasta, being neutral, is a splendid vehicle for fish, meat and vegetable sauces, and also excellent plain, with a little butter or olive oil and grated cheese. I urge my readers to experiment with their own dressing up of all kinds of pasta, bearing in mind that the lighter, thinner variety, such as spaghetti, linguine, little elbows, noodles and so on are suited to light sauces, whereas the thicker kinds, especially the ones with holes, such as rigatoni, need a substantial sauce.

HOW TO MAKE GOOD PASTA ASCIUTTA

Pasta should be cooked al dente: to the toothsome stage, when it is tender yet still resilient to the bite. Overcooked pasta, whatever its shape, is horrible.

To cook pasta properly, it is absolutely essential to have a very big pot with rapidly boiling salted water. Unless the pasta cooks in sufficient water it cannot expand properly and shed its excess starch. Spaghetti, the most popular kind of pasta, also presents the problem of strands sticking together. The addition of a little olive oil to the boiling water helps keep them apart, but this is not necessary (and is seldom done in Italy) when the pasta is stirred properly, as in the step-by-step method that follows.

Another equally important step is to have the pasta reach the table hot, and piping hot at that—the hotter the better. The pasta must be cooked in violently boiling water, drained quickly, poured immediately onto a hot serving dish, served with a sauce that is *hot*, and preferably on really hot dinner plates—as all hot food should be served. If these rules are observed, making good pasta asciutta should present no problem.

How to Cook Spaghetti and Other Pasta

(1) To cook 1 pound, it is essential to have a very large kettle that will hold 6 quarts of water; ½ pound of pasta should be cooked in 3 quarts of water. Add 2 tablespoons salt to 6 quarts water, and 1 tablespoon salt to 3 quarts water.

(2) Bring water to a full, rolling boil. Gradually add spaghetti or other pasta, stirring with a long-handled, two-pronged kitchen fork. The water should keep on boiling hard.

(3) As the pasta begins to soften, fold it over and over in the water so that it won't stick together. Keep on stirring it frequently during the whole cooking process. Lift out a strand occasionally and taste for doneness. Different pastas have different cooking times. The directions on the package provide some indication as to the length of the cooking time, though in general they make for a pasta that is rather over-cooked. Thus tasting is essential to get the pasta right for one's own taste.

Pasta that is to be cooked further in a casserole should not be more than three-quarters done, or the end results will be mushy.

(4) When the pasta is done, drain it immediately into a large strainer or colander. Return to pot and add seasonings. Stir to coat all strands. Serve immediately on heated platter and heated plates.

(5) Never believe that pasta can be cooked in advance (unless for a casserole that will be cooked further). It can't. Never cook pasta until you are ready to eat it. In good

restaurants, insist that it be cooked freshly for you, as it is in Italy.

(6) Pasta *cannot* be reheated, according to Italians.

QUANTITIES TO COOK

Though I've cooked enough pasta to reach several times around the world, I still find it difficult to say exactly how much to cook for a given number of people. It all depends. People of Italian descent will eat more than Anglo-Saxon Americans. Besides, it makes a lot of difference if the pasta dish is the meal itself, with a salad and a dessert, or if it is the first course, to be followed by meat and vegetables.

Pasta swells in cooking. Eight ounces of spaghetti will yield 5 cups cooked; eight ounces of macaroni such as elbows, 4½ cups cooked; eight ounces of egg noodles, 4 cups cooked. Generally, spaghetti and macaroni approximately double in cooking. Small shapes, like sea shells, increase less, and so do noodles.

With all this in mind, I would say—and I don't want to be shot at dawn for the pronouncement—that eight ounces of pasta will feed from two to four people, and one pound from four to six.

Pasta or Rice all'Inglese

(PASTA O RISO ALL'INGLESE)

This is simply a dish of piping hot pasta or rice dressed with butter (preferably sweet butter) and plenty of Parmesan cheese, with pepper to taste. A good quality of spaghetti or other lightweight pasta or homemade noodles, fresh butter and freshly grated cheese make this one of the best dishes ever set before a king.

Macaroni, elbow noodles, lasagne and other heavy-caliber pastas are not suited to this treatment; their substantial nature calls for sauce. The heavier the pasta, the heavier the sauce.

Pasta with Parsley, Garlic and Oil
(PASTA ALL'AGLIO, OLIO E PREZZEMOLO)

I don't think any pasta dish illustrates better than this one how the poorest of the poor in Italy can make an excellent and flavorsome dish out of the simplest ingredients, and the cheapest, relying on the staples of their diet—olive oil, garlic and a green. And strangely enough, this pasta appeals to people with very sophisticated palates.

The amounts of the ingredients depend on one's taste and means. But this is the method. As the pasta is about to finish cooking, warm 1 cup (or more, or less) olive oil in a small saucepan and stir into it as much finely chopped garlic and chopped parsley as you fancy. I like a great deal of parsley and a medium amount of garlic, but opinions on a medium amount of garlic may differ. The oil should be just warm, not hot, and the garlic and parsley should steep in it for 1 to 2 minutes. They should not fry. Toss the whole mixture with the pasta. Cheese can be served with this, and I think it a great improvement, but in Naples, where this pasta is eaten by the poor, cheese is too expensive for them.

Rustic Pasta from Rome

(PASTA RUSTICA DI ROMA)

Like so many Roman dishes, this one starts with a battuto—that is, the mincing together of some of the ingredients on a chopping board

The American way of making a battuto would be to mince each ingredient separately and then combine them all for cooking. The flavor that results, though, is not quite the same; the joint mincing seems to blend the flavors of the ingredients in an inimitable way, which gives the finished dish a subtle though unmistakable character. I shall therefore give the Italian way of making pasta rustica.

1 cup parsley	1 cup bouillon
2 cloves garlic	3 cups shredded cabbage
1 large onion	2 medium-size zucchini,
½ pound bacon	chopped (about 2 cups)
1 large leek	Salt
2 radishes	Pepper
2 medium-size carrots	2 to 3 cups cooked cannellini
3 tablespoons fresh basil	(white kidney beans)
¼ cup olive oil	1 pound rigatoni
3 large tomatoes, peeled,	¼ cup butter
seeded and coarsely	½ cup grated Parmesan
chopped	cheese

On chopping board, mince together parsley, garlic, onion, bacon, leek, radishes, carrots and basil. Heat oil in large kettle and cook mixture in it about 7 minutes, or until soft and just about to brown. Stir frequently. Add tomatoes, bouillon, cabbage, zucchini and salt and pepper. Cover, and cook over low heat 10 to 15 minutes, or until vegetables are tender, stirring frequently. Add cannellini and cook 5 minutes longer.

While vegetables are cooking, cook rigatoni in plenty of rapidly boiling salted water. Drain and toss with butter and cheese. Combine vegetables and pasta and mix thoroughly. Serve with additional grated Parmesan cheese. Serves 6 to 8.

Pasta with Three Cheeses
(LA PASTA CON I TRE FORMAGGI)

Fine dry bread crumbs
1½ tablespoons salt
12 ounces egg noodle bows
(about 6 cups), cooked and
hot
2 tablespoons butter or mar-
garine

1 cup (4 ounces) freshly grated
Parmesan cheese
1 cup (4 ounces) diced Swiss
cheese
1 cup (5 ounces) diced moz-
zarella cheese
3 cups Thin White Sauce
(described below)

Coat a buttered shallow 3-quart baking dish with bread crumbs. Toss noodles with butter, then Parmesan cheese. Add Swiss and mozzarella cheeses; toss lightly. Turn half the noodle mixture into prepared dish; top with half of the Thin White Sauce. Repeat layers. Sprinkle grated Parmesan cheese or bread crumbs on top, if desired. Bake in preheated moderate oven (350° F.) for 25 minutes.

THIN WHITE SAUCE

* To prepare 3 cups: Melt 3 tablespoons butter or margarine in saucepan; blend in 3 tablespoons flour. Gradually add 3 cups milk; cook, stirring constantly, until sauce boils for 1 minute. Add 1½ teaspoons salt, ¼ teaspoon pepper and ⅛ teaspoon nutmeg.

Pasta with Ricotta

(PASTA CON RICOTTA)

The pasta should be very fine noodles, called vermicelli—thin spaghetti, small elbows, small shells, etc. This sauce is for delicate small pasta only.

1 pound (2 cups) ricotta cheese, or more, to taste	Salt
1 cup hot water	Pepper
2 tablespoons melted butter	1 pound thin pasta
2 tablespoons grated Parmesan cheese	

Cream ricotta until fluffy. Gradually stir in the hot water, melted butter and grated Parmesan. Season with salt and pepper to taste. Toss with freshly cooked pasta, making sure the pasta is well coated with the sauce. Serve with additional grated Parmesan, if desired. Makes about 3 cups.

Summer Spaghetti from Ischia

(LA PASTA DI CASAMICCIOLA)

The sauce for this dish is a fresh tomato salad, which is poured over very hot spaghetti or other pasta. There should be an equal quantity of tomatoes and pasta. No grated Parmesan cheese is needed.

Fresh ripe tomatoes, peeled, seeded and coarsely chopped	A little lemon juice
Olive oil	Salt
	Pepper
	Fresh basil

Combine all ingredients and toss well. Add to hot pasta and toss again. Serve immediately.

Spaghetti with Fresh Peas

(SPAGHETTI CON PISELLI)

Another Italian specialty, typical of the way the Italians combine vegetables with pasta. Cut-up eggplant, zucchini, finocchio or broccoli could also be used.

¼ pound Italian prosciutto, or Canadian or other bacon	1 large tomato, peeled, seeded and chopped
1 medium-size onion	2 tablespoons fresh basil
1 clove garlic	Salt
1 3-inch piece celery	Pepper
1 cup parsley	1 pound spaghetti, linguine or other pasta
¼ cup olive oil	
3 tablespoons butter	1 to 2 tablespoons butter
1½ pounds fresh peas, shelled	Grated Parmesan cheese
⅓ cup bouillon	

On chopping board, mince together ham, onion, garlic, celery and parsley. Heat together olive oil and butter. Cook minced vegetables in it over low heat for about 5 minutes. Add peas and bouillon. Cover and simmer until peas are tender, stirring occasionally. Toward the end of the cooking period, add tomato and basil. Season with salt and pepper. If there is too much liquid, cook uncovered to allow for evaporation. The peas should be dry, not soupy.

While peas are cooking, cook pasta in plenty of rapidly boiling salted water. Drain, and toss with vegetables. For a nice touch, add 1 to 2 tablespoons butter. Serve with grated Parmesan cheese.

Spaghetti with Amatriciana Sauce
(SPAGHETTI ALL'AMATRICIANA)

This is a Roman specialty, which must be made with salt pork, lard and plenty of pepper.

¼ pound salt pork	Salt
2 tablespoons lard	¾ teaspoon pepper, or to taste
1 medium onion, thinly sliced	About ⅔ cup each or more
2 to 3 pounds fresh tomatoes,	grated Parmesan and
peeled, seeded and	Romano cheese
chopped	Spaghetti

Soak salt pork in cold water for 5 minutes to remove excess salt. Cut into small dice. Combine pork, lard and onion in a saucepan. Cook over low heat until onion is soft. Add tomatoes, salt and pepper. Cook over high heat, stirring constantly, until the tomatoes are just cooked; they must retain their shape. Serve over spaghetti with grated Parmesan and Romano cheese; there should be plenty of cheese. Enough for 1½ to 2 pounds of spaghetti.

Meatless Sicilian Spaghetti
(SPAGHETTI AL MAGRO ALL'USO DI SIRACUSA)

1 small eggplant	2 tablespoons fresh basil,
Salt	minced, or 1 teaspoon
½ cup olive oil	dried basil
1 garlic clove, minced	2 tablespoons capers
1 small onion, minced	15 pitted black olives, minced
3½ cups plain tomato sauce or	4 anchovy fillets, minced
tomato juice	¼ teaspoon crushed red pepper
¼ cup minced parsley	Spaghetti
1 green pepper, chopped	

Wash eggplant. Cut into ½-inch cubes. Put into a bowl. Sprinkle with salt. Let stand for 1 hour; drain. (This will drain the moisture from the eggplant.) Heat oil in heavy saucepan. Add garlic and onion. Cook, stirring constantly, until onion is soft. Add tomato sauce and simmer, covered, for 10 minutes. Add all remaining ingredients. Check salt; if necessary, add salt to taste. Simmer, covered, over low heat for 30 minutes. Enough for 1½ to 2 pounds spaghetti.

Spaghetti with Carbonara Sauce

(SPAGHETTI ALLA CARBONARA)

Another specialty of popular Roman cookery. Speed is of the essence in preparing this dish. It must be eaten very hot and as soon as it is served to each diner; lukewarm, it loses its character.

6 slices very lean bacon, minced	¼ teaspoon salt
2 tablespoons butter	2 tablespoons minced parsley
1 small onion, minced	⅔ cup grated Parmesan cheese
⅔ cup dry white wine	Freshly ground pepper
3 eggs	Spaghetti

Start cooking spaghetti so that it is ready by the time you finish the sauce. Combine bacon and butter in saucepan. Heat; add onion. Cook, stirring constantly, until onion is soft. Add wine. Cook over high heat until wine has evaporated. Remove from fire, but keep as hot as possible. In a hot serving dish, beat together eggs with salt, parsley, Parmesan cheese and plenty of freshly ground pepper. Drain spaghetti and put immediately into the serving dish with the egg mixture. Toss. Add bacon sauce to it. Toss very well so that the egg-bacon sauce coats all the spaghetti. Serve immediately with additional grated Parmesan cheese. Enough for 1½ to 2 pounds spaghetti.

Note: Carbonara Sauce, like Amatriciana Sauce, is best used on firm long-strand pasta such as spaghetti or linguine.

Green Noodles with Basil

(FETTUCCINE VERDI CON LE ERBE)

1 *pound green noodles*
1 *or 2 garlic cloves, crushed*
1 *cup butter, cut into small pieces*
3 *tablespoons shredded fresh basil leaves, or 2½ teaspoons dried crushed basil leaves (fresh basil is better)*

1 *teaspoon salt*
1 *teaspoon freshly ground black pepper*
½ *cup heavy cream, heated*
1 *cup grated Parmesan or Swiss cheese*

Cook noodles according to package directions. Drain; put into hot serving dish. Toss thoroughly with remaining ingredients until noodles are well coated. Serve immediately on very hot plates.

Homemade Pasta

(PASTA FATTA IN CASA)

Many Italian women, especially in the South, make their own pasta daily because it is much less expensive than buying it. And for flavor, nothing beats homemade pasta; restaurants have based their reputations on the excellence of their home-made noodles. People who frequently make their own pasta at home should invest in a home rolling-and-cutting machine; these can be bought in houseware stores that go in for imports. The pasta dough can be used for ravioli, cannelloni, etc.

4 cups sifted all-purpose flour　　*About ¼ cup cold water*
2 teaspoons salt　　　　　　　　*Flour for flouring board*
3 eggs, lightly beaten

On a floured baking board, sift together flour and salt into the shape of a pyramid. Make a well in the center. Pour beaten eggs into well. Mix flour and eggs together gradually with the right hand. With the left hand, add the cold water a very little at a time as you go on mixing with the right hand. Add just enough water to make a firm dough that is barely soft enough to handle. Sprinkle a little flour on the baking board. Turn dough on it and knead for 10 to 15 minutes, using both hands and rolling the ball of dough to and fro. If necessary, sprinkle a little more flour on the baking board to prevent sticking. Knead noodle dough until it is elastic and perfectly smooth. Divide dough into 4 parts. Flour board again. Roll out one piece of dough at a time with a floured rolling pin. Stretch the dough with the pin until it is between ¹⁄₁₆ and ⅛ of an inch thick; this will make a light flouring of the rolling pin and of the board necessary when-ever the dough tends to stick to them. Roll up each sheet of dough loosely for cutting. For noodles or fettucine, slice the roll in widths of about ¼ inch; for lasagne, into 1½-inch strips, and the strips into 6-inch lengths. Put a clean tablecloth or paper toweling on a table. Spread the pasta on it. Let stand to dry out for about 1 hour before cooking. Drop into boiling salt water. Cook for about 5 minutes or until just tender. Drain and serve with butter and grated Parmesan, or with a sauce. Makes about 1 pound of pasta, or enough for 4 people.

Homemade Noodles Alfredo

(FETTUCCINE ALLA ALFREDO)

The original Alfredo was an excellent restaurateur who ran a famous restaurant in the old Roman street alla Scrofa—that is, the Street of the Sow (shown on an antique frieze that used to be there). He was also a born ham, and his customers loved it. He used to celebrate this noodle dish—there is no other word for it—with a golden spoon and fork, tossing the noodles with a flourish.

This noodle dish is excellent, even when made with "boughten" noodles. The trick is to use equal parts of noodles, butter and freshly ground Parmesan cheese and to have everything extremely hot. Also, *the butter must not be melted.* When made with first-class ingredients, this is one of the great noodle dishes of all times.

1 pound broad noodles (pref-
erably homemade)
1 pound sweet butter (it must
be sweet butter), cut in
slices

1 pound Parmesan cheese (it
must be freshly grated)

Cook noodles al dente. Drain and put into a big, very hot bowl. Add the butter slices and cheese. Toss very thoroughly so that the noodles are evenly coated. Serve immediately on very hot plates.

Green Lasagne alla Bolognese

(LASAGNE VERDI ALLA BOLOGNESE)

Lasagne are extra-wide and rather heavy noodles, which sometimes have crimped edges. Like all noodle products, they are good, but even better when homemade. The dough is a noodle

dough, made green with puréed spinach—just like the com-
mercially produced green noodles.

The Bolognese part comes in with the sauces used in this
lasagne dish. There are a great many ways of making lasagne
creations: with meat sauces, meat balls, shrimps, all with or
without several cheeses such as mozzarella, ricotta and Parmesan. I think the Bolognese way is best, because it is less
lethal than those that stem from the heavy Southern Italian
cuisine, which is full of herbs, spices and tomatoes.

Bologna is the eating capital of Italy. This is an incredible
city of block-long private houses and fortress walls, towers,
arcades, great churches and squares of a truly theatrical
splendor. It is also the home of the oldest European and most
famous Italian university (which has earned her the title of
La Dotta, the Learned One). Its cuisine of noodle products
(and others, but this is not the chapter for them) is pure
poetry.

As a friend of mine put it when we were watching a
plump lady making tortellini, tiny stuffed noodle rings, with
a skill and speed that must be inborn: "La cucina bolognese fa
sorrideri gli angeli in paradiso [Bolognese cooking makes the
angels in paradise smile]."

Bolognese meat sauces are made with lean beef, veal and
pork, with chicken livers, and with marrow, tenderly pointed
up with herbs, seasonings, very little tomato, and with wine
and truffles. The white sauce that goes into this lasagne dish is
well seasoned with nutmeg, another favorite of the city's
cooking. It takes time to make Lasagne Verdi alla Bolognese,
but the effort is well worth it, especially since the dish can be
prepared for a large number of people, and beforehand as
well. Lasagne can be stored in the refrigerator, or frozen. It
can be made with the bought variety, but since homemade
green lasagne are rightfully considered to be very glamorous,
I give the recipe. Essentially, it is noodle dough made green,
and if my patient reader has a pet homemade noodles recipe,

I advise her to follow it, adding the puréed spinach to the dough while decreasing the quantity of the liquid used, be it beaten egg or water.

The spinach must be cooked and must retain its fresh green color. It must be puréed very fine—either by pressing through a sieve or in a blender. And, furthermore, the spinach must be thoroughly drained before being mixed into the dough. If it is still wet, heat it for a moment over high heat to evaporate some of the moisture, stirring constantly. This dough is also good for noodles, ravioli and the like.

4 cups sifted flour
2 teaspoons salt
3 eggs, well beaten

½ pound extremely finely puréed spinach

Sift flour and salt into a large bowl. Make a well in the center and put eggs and spinach in it. Mix gradually with one hand or stir with a fork until the paste is well blended. Since flours vary in their absorption of liquid, in order to obtain a smooth paste you may have to add a little water if the paste is too stiff (1 tablespoon at a time) or a little more flour if it is too wet. Go easy on the flour, adding 1 tablespoon at a time, or the lasagne will be heavy. Knead the dough thoroughly for at least 12 minutes, pushing it away from you on the board with the palms of both hands. Also take the ball of dough in both hands and pummel it hard, banging it on the board until it is thoroughly smooth and elastic. (This banging noise is very characteristic of Italian kitchens.) The dough must be dry and not cling to your hands. If it does, flour your hands lightly and work the flour into the dough.

Let the dough rest for 15 to 30 minutes after it has reached the right elasticity. Divide it into 4 pieces. Flour the board and the rolling pin lightly (you will need more flour before you are through, and the less you use for each flouring the better for your lasagne) and roll the dough to about ⅟₁₆ of an inch thick. As you do so, stretch it around the rolling pin, pulling the dough toward the handles to get it thinner. Lightly flour the flattened paste after each rolling to keep it from sticking. By the time the dough has been rolled and stretched about a dozen times it should be the texture of a piece of cloth which can be folded and manipulated without breaking. Put the pasta sheets that are ready on a clean kitchen towel on the table or hang them over the back of a chair while you are working on the other ones.

Cut the prepared dough into strips 2 by 4 to 6 or 8 inches, depending on the size of the dish in which the lasagne is to be baked. Let them dry on towels for about 1 hour. Boil the strips a few at a time in plenty of rapidly boiling salted water for 3 to 5 minutes, or until almost but not quite tender. Remove them from the kettle and drop in cold salted water. Drain them again and dry them by spreading on kitchen towels.

Butter a 2-quart baking dish. Coat the bottom with a small amount of Ragú alla Bolognese, a small amount of cream sauce and a sprinkling of grated Parmesan cheese. Place a layer of lasagne on this base, with the ends turning up at the sides of the dish. Repeat this procedure, ending with meat sauce, cream sauce and a generous layer of Parmesan cheese. Bake in a moderate (350° F.) oven 20 to 25 minutes, or until the lasagne is golden brown and very hot, and the cheese melted. Cut into wedges.

Note: This recipe makes about 1½ pounds of lasagne. Since you may want to make extra noodle dough while you are at it, *here are the quantities of sauces and cheese needed for each ¾ to 1 pound of lasagne.*

3 cups Italian meat sauce from Bologna or any other meat sauce

2½ cups white sauce or cream sauce

¾ cup grated Parmesan cheese

Three-fourths to 1 pound lasagne and the above quantities of sauces and cheese will fill one 8-inch-square baking pan.

Cannelloni Filling

Cannelloni means big rolls in Italian, and any rolls made from dough can be filled and baked. There is the store-bought variety of cannelloni: big (that is, about 4 inches long and rather thick). There are also cannelloni made from egg-noodle dough (more elegant) and (most elegant) cannelloni made from baked French pancakes, cut, like the egg-noodle dough, into 4-inch squares. All of these can be filled with any savory or creamy mixture, sauced up and baked. Restaurants that specialize in cannelloni usually compose their cannelloni sauce from three, four or more sauces, which are combined and seasoned again. This is obviously not feasible for the home cook. The following recipe is, however, feasible and good. It can be dolled up further according to the whim of the cook with some sautéed sliced mushrooms, a few chopped truffles, a touch of brandy and/or any seasonings she fancies. The filling stuffs over 24 cannelloni, depending on size, and serves 8 to 12.

3 chicken breasts, skinned and boned	½ cup flour
¾ cup butter	4 cups hot milk
6 large chicken livers	1 cup heavy cream
8 slices Italian prosciutto or cooked ham	Salt
2 cups grated Swiss or Parmesan cheese	Pepper
	¼ teaspoon nutmeg

In a heavy skillet, sauté chicken breasts in ¼ cup of the butter over medium heat for about 10 to 15 minutes, or until golden brown. Push to one side of the skillet and sauté chicken livers for 3 to 4 minutes. Grind chicken breasts, livers, and prosciutto together, using the finest blade of the meat grinder. Blend in 1 cup of the cheese.

Over low heat or in the top of a double boiler, melt remaining butter and stir in the flour. Cook 2 to 3 minutes. Blend in hot milk, stirring constantly. Cook 10 minutes, stirring frequently, or until thick and smooth. Add heavy cream, salt and pepper to taste, and nutmeg. Add about 1 cup of the sauce to the chicken mixture and blend thoroughly. Stuff cannelloni with this mixture. If noodle dough squares are used, they must first be boiled in rapidly boiling salted water until tender, drained and dried on a kitchen towel.

The noodle or pancake squares are stuffed by placing about 2 tablespoons of filling on each square and rolling it tightly. Arrange cannelloni in buttered shallow baking dishes one layer deep—no more. Sprinkle with remaining cheese and a little of the remaining sauce. Dot cannelloni with additional butter and bake in preheated moderate (350° F.) oven until the tops are golden brown. Serve very hot, with a tossed or a green cooked vegetable salad on the side.

Ravioli

Ravioli may be served all'inglese, that is, with butter and grated Parmesan cheese, or with a meat or tomato sauce. There is also a kind of tiny ravioli, called tortellini, which are served in consommé. These are a specialty of Bologna, home of the best Italian ravioli.

Basic Homemade Pasta (page 70)
Filling (page 78)

Make pasta according to directions, but divide into 2 parts only. Roll out half of the dough on a lightly floured board to an oblong of about 10 by 16 inches. Put small teaspoons of filling on the dough at the distance of 2 inches from each other. Roll out the remaining half of the dough and brush with water. Put dough, water side down, on the filling. Firmly press the edges of the dough around each teaspoon of filling. With a sharp knife or a pastry jagger, cut the ravioli into 2-inch squares. Let dry for about 2 hours. Cook ravioli in rapidly boiling salted water until tender. Serve with butter and grated cheese or a spaghetti or tomato sauce.

RAVIOLI FILLINGS

Any ravioli filling should be finely textured and very compact, so that it won't ooze out of its protective dough shell during cooking. The fine texture is achieved by grinding meats twice and working them with the other ingredients into a cohesive mixture.

A ravioli mixture should be well seasoned; since one ravioli is a tiny morsel, the filling has to be tasty to be noticed and remembered. There really is no set rule as to what can go into a filling; ravioli cooks and restaurants famous for their ravioli have their secret combinations. A ravioli filling may also be used for stuffing the thick kinds of pasta, such as rigatoni.

Enthusiastic ravioli makers would do well to invest in a special pan with a number of little indentures (a kind of miniature muffin pan) which speeds up the job and makes for symmetrical ravioli. This pan can be bought in fancy houseware stores or stores with imported Italian housewares.

Ravioli Filling with Mixed Meats

(RAVIOLI CON LE CARNI DIVERSE)

⅔ cup ground cooked
    prosciutto (fat and lean)
    or bacon
1 cup ground raw white
    chicken meat
1 cup ground cooked veal
2 egg yolks
1 teaspoon salt

½ teaspoon pepper
Grated rind of ½ large lemon
⅛ teaspoon ground nutmeg
1 tablespoon olive oil
¼ cup grated Parmesan cheese
1 tablespoon minced parsley
Fine dry breadcrumbs

Combine all ingredients except breadcrumbs. Blend well to make a smooth mixture. If mixture is too soft, add breadcrumbs, a little at a time, such as a teaspoon or less. Do not overload with breadcrumbs. Makes about 3¼ cups filling.

Meatless Ravioli with Ricotta

(RAVIOLI DI MAGRO CON RICOTTA)

1 pound (2 cups) ricotta cheese
2 tablespoons grated Parmesan
    cheese
1 tablespoon minced parsley
1 teaspoon grated lemon rind

⅛ teaspoon ground nutmeg
½ teaspoon salt
⅛ teaspoon pepper
1 egg yolk, beaten

Combine all ingredients. Mix to make a smooth mixture.

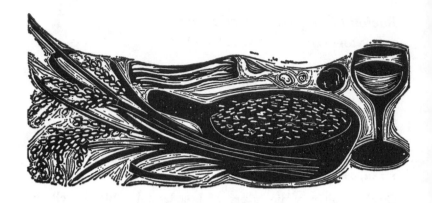

RICE

NORTHERN ITALY, that is, the Piedmont, Lombardy and the Veneto, eat rice as their staple starch, the way, in the South, spaghetti and pastas are eaten daily. There are various kinds of short- and long-grained rice that grow in the risaie, the endless rice fields of Northern Italy. An unforgettable sight is the Lombard plain, as flat as a pancake, with its watery rice fields divided by Lombardy poplars, interspersed with mulberry trees, these to feed the silkworms for Milan's and Como's world-famous silk mills.

What makes Italian rice dishes, or risotto—that is, a big rice—different from those of the Greeks, Arabs, Spaniards, Turks and Persians is that the rice is creamy, with a very slight resistant heart to each grain. Thus, the texture of risotto is lovely, both creamy and chewy at the same time. I have never been able to achieve this creaminess with rice other than

Italian rice. Our Carolina rice, both long- and short-grained, will come close; the converted rice, perfect as it is for dry pilafs, does not lend itself to Italian risottos.

The secret of some Italian rice cookery is that the rice is cooked—I am talking of a classic Milanese risotto—in a small amount of liquid at a time. You stand over the pot, ladling in the hot broth or liquid slowly, and only when the rice is on the verge of sticking to the pot. Of course, you must stir all the time, but the results are worth it.

In Italy, rice is never served as a side dish or as a vegetable, with the single exception of Ossobuco, veal shanks, which come with a risotto alla Milanese. Otherwise, whatever fish, meat or vegetables go with the rice are cooked right into it to make a first course.

Risotto alla Milanese

What makes Risotto alla Milanese different from other risotto is saffron. It may be served plain or with sautéed chicken livers, mushrooms, truffles and any savory sauce. The sauce, though, must be kept on the delicate side—no heavy meat-tomato mixtures—or the delicate risotto will be drowned in the alien flavor.

¼ cup butter
¼ cup chopped beef marrow
    (if marrow is unavailable,
    use 2 tablespoons butter
    instead)
¼ cup very finely minced
    onion
2 cups raw Carolina or Italian
    rice

½ cup Marsala or dry white
    wine
About 5 cups boiling chicken
    bouillon
½ to ¾ teaspoon saffron,
    steeped in a little chicken
    broth
3 tablespoons butter
⅔ cup Parmesan cheese

In heavy saucepan, melt butter and beef marrow. Over medium heat, cook onion in it until golden but not brown. Add the unwashed rice, stirring constantly until it becomes transparent in about 3 to 4 minutes. The rice must not brown. Stir in Marsala. When the wine has evaporated, add ½ cup of the bouillon, which is kept boiling hot in a separate saucepan. Cook over medium heat, uncovered, until the bouillon is absorbed. Stir constantly. Add the rest of the bouillon gradually, as the rice absorbs it, stirring constantly. The less bouillon added at a time, the better the rice. The cooking time should be around 20 minutes from the time the stock is first added, and the stirring constant.

After about 15 minutes' cooking time, or before the rice is tender, add the saffron. When the rice is cooked, stir in the 2 tablespoons butter and the grated Parmesan cheese. Serve immediately and very hot, with additional Parmesan.

Note: Instead of using ½ cup Marsala and about 5 cups chicken broth, you can make a lighter risotto with 1 cup dry white wine and 4½ cups chicken broth. Please note also that the amount of liquid must be gauged as the rice is cooking, since various kinds of rice absorb different amounts of liquid. The result should be a rice that is creamy but not sloppy.

White Risotto with Mushrooms

(RISO IN BIANCO CON FUNGHI)

A white risotto, that is, one without tomatoes or any other ingredient that would color the rice, is a classic of Italian cookery. The rice should be creamy, but still al dente, or chewy.

¼ cup olive oil
1 whole garlic clove
½ pound mushrooms, thinly
  sliced
½ cup minced parsley
Salt
Pepper

¼ cup butter
½ medium onion, thinly sliced
1½ cups long-grain Carolina
  rice
4 cups hot chicken broth
½ cup dry white wine
½ cup grated Parmesan cheese

Heat olive oil and garlic clove. Add mushrooms and parsley. Season lightly with salt and pepper. Cook over medium heat, stirring constantly, for about 5 minutes, or until mushrooms are almost tender. Remove from heat and take out and throw away garlic clove; reserve mushrooms. Heat butter in 2-quart casserole. Add onion and cook, over low heat, until onion is soft but still white. Add rice. Cook over medium heat, stirring constantly, about 2 minutes or until rice is opaque. Add hot chicken broth ¼ cup at a time, stirring constantly. When the rice has absorbed the broth, add more. Stir constantly to prevent scorching. Add wine. When rice is creamy and almost cooked, add mushrooms. Since different kinds of rice absorb liquids differently, a little more hot broth may be needed. Add it a tablespoon at a time. Cook together until mushrooms and rice are tender. Stir in Parmesan cheese and serve hot.

Note: For a finer risotto, add a thinly sliced white Italian truffle, fresh or canned. This is wonderful.

White Risotto with Zucchini, Artichokes or Other Vegetables

The principle is the same as in White Risotto with Mushrooms. The vegetables are sliced and sautéed in oil or butter with a little parsley and garlic, if desired, until almost done.

Then the white risotto is made. Rice and vegetables are combined to cook together until tender.

Venetian Risotto and Peas

(RISI E BISI)

One of the famous dishes of Venice, and one of the best of the scores of northern Italian risotti. For 4 to 6 people.

½ cup butter	1½ cups unwashed rice
1 medium-size onion, finely minced	3½ cups hot chicken bouillon
	Salt
2 slices prosciutto or ham, chopped	Pepper
	½ cup grated Parmesan cheese
4 cups shelled or frozen peas	

In heavy saucepan, heat butter. Cook onion and prosciutto in it over medium heat for about 5 minutes, or until golden, stirring frequently. Add peas and cook 5 minutes longer. Stir in rice and cook until transparent—about 4 to 5 minutes, stirring constantly. Add hot chicken bouillon and salt and pepper to taste. Cover saucepan and cook over low heat for 15 to 20 minutes, stirring frequently. The rice should absorb all the liquid and be tender but not mushy. Stir in Parmesan cheese and serve very hot, with additional Parmesan.

Country Risotto
(RISOTTO RUSTICO)

1 cup dry white beans or pea
　　beans
4 cups well-flavored bouillon
2 medium potatoes, cut into
　　½-inch cubes
2 large carrots, sliced
2 artichokes, thinly sliced
2 zucchini squash, sliced
2 leeks, white and green parts,
　　sliced

1 turnip, cut into ½-inch cubes
1½ cups raw long-grain rice
2 pounds fresh peas, shelled
Salt
Pepper
½ cup butter
½ teaspoon ground sage or 2 to
　　4 dried or fresh sage leaves
Grated Parmesan cheese

Pour boiling water over beans and let stand 1 hour. In deep
kettle, cook beans with additional water to cover, until three-
quarters done. Add 3 cups of the bouillon and bring to a boil.
Add vegetables. Cook over high heat for about 4 minutes. Add
rice and remaining bouillon. Cook, covered, over medium
heat, stirring frequently, until rice is almost tender. Add peas.
Season with salt and pepper. Cook, covered, until peas are
tender. If risotto is too liquid, cook without cover to allow for
evaporation. Melt butter and add sage to it. Stir butter into
risotto. Serve with freshly grated Parmesan cheese. Serves
6 to 8.

Note: This dish may be also made into a thick soup. Just
add more hot bouillon for desired consistency. Serves 6.

Venetian Risotto with Chicken
(RISOTTO ALLA SBIRRAGLIA)

1 2½- to 3-pound chicken
6 to 7 cups water
2 small onions
1 medium carrot
½ stalk celery
1 medium leek (optional)
Salt
Pepper

1 to 2 tablespoons minced
blanched salt pork or
bacon
¼ cup butter
½ cup dry white wine
1 tablespoon tomato paste
2 cups long-grain Carolina rice
Grated Parmesan cheese

Cut chicken meat from bones and skin. Remove all fat and cut meat into thin strips. Chop chicken liver and gizzard. In a deep kettle, put water, chicken bones and neck, 1 of the onions, the carrot, celery and leek. Season with salt and pepper. Bring to a boil and skim. Simmer, covered, for about ¾ hour to make chicken broth, skimming as needed. Strain broth and throw away bones. On chopping board, mince together the remaining onion and the salt pork to make a paste. Combine mixture and butter in a 3-quart casserole. Cook over medium heat, stirring constantly, for about 3 minutes. Add chicken, chicken liver and gizzard. Cook, stirring constantly, for 3 to 5 minutes, or until slightly golden. Add wine and tomato paste. Mix well. Simmer, covered, over low heat for about 10 minutes. Stir frequently. Measure 6 cups of broth and heat. Add rice and broth to chicken mixture. Simmer, covered, stirring frequently for about 20 minutes or until the rice is tender and has absorbed all the liquid. Check for moisture. If too dry, add a little more broth or water; if too liquid, cook, uncovered, to allow for evaporation.

Fregoli's Risotto

(RISOTTO ALLA FREGOLI)

A rich and exquisite Roman dish created in honor of Fregoli, a variety artist famous for the fancifulness of his tricks and the speed with which he did them.

½ ounce dried imported mush-
    rooms
½ cup water
1 sweetbread
Water
1 teaspoon lemon juice
¼ pound chicken livers
¼ pound prosciutto or
    Canadian bacon
¾ cup butter
½ small onion, thinly sliced

½ cup dry white wine
½ cup Marsala
2 cups uncooked rice
1 truffle, sliced
3 cups beef consommé
1 cup shelled peas or frozen
    peas, thawed
Salt
Pepper
⅔ cup grated Parmesan cheese

Cut mushrooms into pieces and steep in water. Steep sweetbread in cold water for 1 hour, changing water several times. Put into saucepan. Cover with water to which lemon juice has been added. Slowly bring to a boil. Cook, uncovered, for 3 minutes. Drain; plunge into cold water. Drain again. Cut off cartilage, tubes, connective tissue and tough membrane. Cut into ½-inch cubes. Trim fat off chicken livers and cut into halves, or, if very large, into quarters. Cut prosciutto into julienne strips. Drain mushrooms and reserve liquid. Heat half of the butter in heavy saucepan or casserole. Add onion, mushrooms, sweetbread, chicken livers and prosciutto. Cook over medium heat, stirring constantly, for about 3 minutes or until golden brown. Add mushroom liquid, wine, Marsala, rice and truffle. Cook over medium heat, stirring frequently, until the wines have been absorbed by the rice. Lower heat. Stir in beef consommé. Simmer, covered, over lowest possible heat for 10 to 15 minutes, or until rice is almost tender. Stir frequently. Add peas and salt and pepper to taste. Simmer, covered, until rice is cooked and on the dry side. Stir in remaining butter and half of the grated Parmesan cheese. Put into serving dish and sprinkle with remaining Parmesan cheese.

Note: The different kinds of rice absorb liquids differently. Check for moisture; add a little more bouillon if needed, or cook, uncovered, to allow for evaporation.

Rita's Rice and Vegetable Entree

(LA TEGLIA DI RITA)

Rita, my mother's caretaker at our house on Lake Maggiore, served this dish before a course of meat and salad, followed by cheese and fruit.

2 cups uncooked rice	*1½ cups grated Parmesan*
2 medium eggplants (about 1	*cheese*
to 1½ pounds)	*2 pounds tomatoes, sliced*
2 tablespoons salt	*1 cup chopped parsley*
1 pound zucchini	*2 teaspoons dried basil leaves,*
1 teaspoon salt	*crushed*
½ cup olive oil	*Pepper*
2 garlic cloves	*2 tablespoons butter*

Cook rice in boiling salted water until three-quarters done. Drain. Peel eggplants. Cut into ½-inch cubes. Place in bowl and sprinkle with salt. Let stand for ½ to 1 hour, to shed excess liquid. Cut zucchini into ½-inch cubes. Heat olive oil and garlic. Fry zucchini in hot oil for 3 minutes; they must remain crisp. Drain on kitchen paper and sprinkle with 1 teaspoon salt. Drain eggplant thoroughly. Fry in the same olive oil in which the zucchini was fried, for 3 minutes. Drain on paper towels. Remove garlic cloves and throw away. Thoroughly butter a deep 3-quart baking dish. Put in alternate layers of rice, Parmesan cheese, parsley, basil, eggplant, zucchini and sliced tomatoes. Season each layer with pepper. End with a layer of tomatoes and cheese. Dot with butter. Bake in preheated moderate oven (350° F.) for 45 minutes to 1 hour or until thoroughly heated. Makes 8 to 10 servings. Equally good hot or cold.

Rice Timbale

(TIMBALLO DI RISO)

A handsome and ornamental creation of Milanese cooking, well suited to buffet suppers.

2⅔ cups raw Carolina or Italian rice	⅓ cup grated Parmesan cheese
½ cup butter	4 egg yolks
	Fine dry bread crumbs

Cook rice in salted water until tender. Drain. Mix in the ½ cup butter, Parmesan cheese, and egg yolks. Butter a 3-quart casserole and sprinkle with fine dry bread crumbs. (The casserole must be thoroughly coated.)

Spoon two-thirds of the rice mixture into the casserole. Press rice against bottom and sides, leaving a well in the middle. Put filling in the well. Spoon the remaining rice over the top of the entire casserole, taking care that the meat is well covered. Bake uncovered in moderate (350° F.) oven about 1 hour, or until rice is set. Unmold on a heated platter. Cut into wedges and serve with tomato sauce. Makes 8 to 10 servings.

FILLING

2 tablespoons butter	*1½ cups cooked peas*
¼ cup finely minced onion	*4 tablespoons tomato paste*
1 clove garlic, finely minced	*flavored with basil leaf*
1 pound veal and pork mixed,	*1 teaspoon salt*
ground twice	*1 teaspoon sugar*
½ pound raw chicken livers,	*½ teaspoon oregano*
chopped	*¼ teaspoon black pepper*
⅓ cup pimiento	

Melt 2 tablespoons butter in a skillet. Add onion and garlic. Cook over low heat until onion is golden and transparent. Add ground meat and chicken livers. Cook, stirring occasionally, for about 15 minutes, or until meats are tender. Add pimiento, cooked peas, tomato paste, salt, sugar, oregano and pepper. Cook over low heat for about 20 minutes, stirring frequently.

Rice Croquettes with Mozzarella

(SUPPLÌ AL TELEFONO)

A Roman specialty, which is sold in all the wine shops as the perfect companion for a glass of wine. Many students lived on supplì as a daily diet, spending their food money on other, less public amusements. The "telefono" bit refers to the mozzarella, which in Italy (where it is somewhat different from ours) dissolves into strings when cooked. Supplì make a good dish, utilizing leftover rice.

2 cups cooked rice
½ cup grated Parmesan or
  Romano cheese
1 egg, well beaten
1 tablespoon melted butter
1 teaspoon salt

⅛ teaspoon pepper
½-inch cubes of mozzarella
  cheese
Bread crumbs
Olive oil or shortening for deep
  frying

Combine rice and grated cheese and mix well. Stir in egg,
butter, salt and pepper. Cover each mozzarella cube with rice
and shape into 2-inch balls or croquettes. Make sure the cheese
is well covered, so that it won't ooze out during frying. Coat
cheese balls with bread crumbs. Fry in deep hot fat (365° F.)
for 5 to 8 minutes, or until golden brown on all sides. Drain
on paper towels. Makes 12 to 16 croquettes, depending on
their size.

CORNMEAL
AND DUMPLINGS

POLENTA IS YELLOW CORNMEAL, and one of the staple foods of Northern Italy, especially in Lombardy and in the country around Venice. The cornmeal, also called yellow flour or farina gialla, comes ground in various degrees of fineness; our own cornmeal resembles the fine polenta. The others are more coarsely ground, and, to my mind, far tastier. White cornmeal is not known in Italy.

Polenta, like all cornmeal, must always be boiled first in plenty of water, and stirred constantly. It is then eaten hot, with a sauce such as spaghetti sauces that may contain meat, cheese, fish, especially cod, or simply with boiled chestnuts or with milk. Or else, polenta is sliced and used in place of bread. There are also dishes made with polenta, such as pies (polenta pasticciata), a rich filling of ham, cheese, mushrooms and what not. Polenta e iirei, that is, polenta with roasted tiny song birds, is a famous dish from Bergamo; fortunately, unlike Italy, America does not allow their wholesale slaughter.

Finally, like all cornmeal mush, cold polenta may be sliced and fried in a little oil or butter.

The secret of a good polenta is to cook the cornmeal for a long time, stirring it constantly; old-fashioned cookery books say for 45 minutes to 1 hour. One of the signs of sufficiently cooked polenta is a delicious crisp crust clinging to the sides of the dish in which it was cooked.

In Northern Italy, especially in the country, polenta is cooked in a deep copper kettle called paiuolo and stirred with a wooden paddle. The kettle used to be hung from a hook over the large open fireplace; now, it sits on a gas or wood stove. Traditionally, polenta is never cut with a knife. The cooked cornmeal is turned out on a wooden board keeping the shape of the kettle, and cut into thick slices with a string.

Basic Polenta

Polenta, ground coarsely or more finely, can be found in all Italian grocery stores. The amount of water will have to be adjusted depending on the grind used; coarser polenta needs more water. The following recipe has been adapted to yellow American cornmeal. The double-boiler method avoids much of the constant stirring.

1 cup yellow cornmeal   *1 teaspoon salt*
4 cups water

Mix cornmeal with 1½ cups of the water to a smooth paste. Pour remaining water and salt into the top of a double boiler.

Bring to a boil. Gradually add cornmeal paste to boiling water, stirring constantly. Cook over medium heat, stirring constantly, until mixture boils. Put double boiler pot over boiling water. Cook, covered, stirring frequently, for about 45 minutes. Turn out on board. Makes about 4 cups.

Baked Polenta with Mushrooms
(LA POLENTA PASTICCIATA CON I FUNGHI)

A good supper dish.

¼ cup olive oil	½ teaspoon salt
1 medium onion, minced	¼ teaspoon pepper
1 garlic clove, minced	8 cups cooked polenta, hot
2 tablespoons minced parsley	½ cup butter
¾ to 1 pound mushrooms, sliced	1 cup grated Parmesan cheese
⅔ cup canned tomatoes	

In deep skillet, heat olive oil. Add onion, garlic clove and parsley. Cook, stirring constantly, until onion is soft. Add mushrooms and tomatoes. Cook over medium heat for 7 to 10 minutes, or until mushrooms are cooked, but still firm. Season with salt and pepper.

Make Basic Polenta (page 93) but double the quantity. While polenta is hot, beat in ¼ cup of the butter and the grated Parmesan cheese. Put polenta into a 9-by-5-by- 3-inch loaf pan and cool. Remove cooled polenta from loaf pan. Cut into 2 parts. Return 1 part to loaf pan. Cover with mushroom sauce. Top with remaining polenta. Dot with remaining butter. Bake in preheated moderate oven (350° F.) for 30 minutes, or until top is golden brown and crusty. Serve with a tossed green salad.

Polenta with Cheese
(IL "TÔCC")

This is a specialty of the country around Lake Como; a polenta dressed with much butter and cheese, and very good. The cheese should be one that melts easily, such as a Fontina or a Bel Paese; around Como they use skim milk, "fresh," that is, unaged, local cheese. For a different taste, mozzarella may be used. The tôcc is served as is as a main dish, or with milk on the side.

Use equal quantities of butter, cheese and hot cooked polenta. Have butter and cheese at room temperature. Cut into ½-inch cubes. Keep polenta over lowest possible heat. Work in, stirring constantly, alternate cubes of butter and cheese. The polenta should be one smooth mixture, with no visible pieces of butter or cheese. Eat warm or cold.

Roman Dumplings
(GNOCCHI ALLA ROMANA)

The Italian word gnocco means a dumpling when applied to food and a dope when applied to a person. This recipe makes an excellent substitute for potatoes, rice or pasta, and a delightful main dish for luncheon or supper.

1½ cups water	½ cup butter
1½ cups milk	3 eggs
1 cup farina or Cream of Wheat	2 cups (½ pound) grated Parmesan or Swiss cheese (Parmesan preferred)
1½ teaspoons salt	

Bring milk and water to a boil. Gradually stir in farina and salt, taking care to avoid lumping. Cook over medium heat until thick. Remove from heat. Beat in ¼ cup of the butter, ½ cup cheese and the eggs, and mix well. Spread about ¼ inch thick on a shallow platter or on a cooky sheet. Cool. With the rim of a glass or a cooky cutter cut into circles or any desired shapes. Arrange in buttered baking dish in overlapping layers. Sprinkle each layer with the remaining 1½ cups cheese and ¼ cup butter. Bake in preheated moderate (350° F.) oven about 30 minutes, or until golden and crisp.

Note: This dish can be prepared well in advance, stored in refrigerator, and baked when needed.

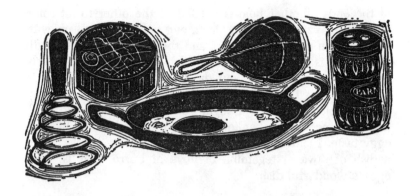

EGGS AND CHEESE

A GREAT MANY EGGS are eaten in Italy, but never at breakfast, unless some snob wants to imitate British and American breakfast habits. Eggs are luncheon and supper food, but Italian egg cookery is very simple. Most eggs are eaten al tegamino, that is, fried in butter or olive oil in individual little two-handled frying pans, and they are served in the pan to keep them hot. Uova strapazzate, scrambled eggs, or literally, utterly fatigued eggs, are less popular than fried ones. Omelets, or frittate, on the other hand, are extremely popular, especially with the addition of vegetables, meats, fish or leftovers, because they make a little go a long way.

To this day, a great many Italians believe in the building-up properties of raw eggs. There are various ways of presenting a raw egg. It can be sucked through a hole made at one of the ends (another hole is needed at the other to let some air in to make it suckable). Or an egg yolk is beaten up with a tablespoon of sugar in a cup, and the cup is then filled with coffee; this is a frequent breakfast drink, especially for elderly or delicate people, and about the only way the egg figures in the indigenous Italian breakfast. Or an egg yolk is beaten up with a tablespoon each of sugar and Marsala as invalid food, a sort of uncooked zabaglione, and quite good if one likes an eggy taste. Incidentally, a slice or two of white truffle makes a dish of uova al tegamino or uova al burro, that is, fried eggs, a wonderful dish.

Italian Omelets
(FRITTATE)

These are not at all soft inside like French omelets. Italian omelets are rather like flat cakes, resembling a pancake. They are generally cooked on both sides, and served cut into flat wedges. Very often, cooked leftover vegetables and/or meats are added to the egg mixture, to cook with it. Or an onion or another vegetable may be quickly sautéed in butter or olive oil, before the addition of the eggs.

Tuna Fish Omelet
(FRITTATA DI TONNO)

4 eggs, beaten
¼ teaspoon pepper
1 tablespoon chopped parsley
½ teaspoon dried basil or any other herb

1 medium (7 ounces) can tuna, drained and chopped fine
2 anchovy fillets (optional), minced
3 tablespoons olive oil

Combine all ingredients except olive oil. Mix well. Heat oil
in frying pan. Add egg mixture and cook over low heat for
about 5 to 7 minutes on each side. Turn over once.

Mozzarella and Bread Cubes Omelet

(FRITTATA CON MOZZARELLA E CROSTINI)

6 eggs, slightly beaten
¾ teaspoon salt
¼ teaspoon pepper
4 ounces (½ package) mozza-
    rella cheese, diced

4 slices firm white bread
⅓ cup butter

Combine eggs, salt, pepper and mozzarella. Trim crusts from
bread and cut into ¼-inch cubes. Heat butter in skillet. Fry
bread cubes in it until golden and crisp. Add egg mixture.
Cook over low heat for about 5 minutes. Turn on other side
and cook until set. Serve immediately.

Zucchini Omelet

(FRITTATA DI ZUCCHINE)

2 zucchini, sliced
Flour for dredging
3 tablespoons olive oil
4 to 6 eggs, slightly beaten
1 tablespoon grated Parmesan
    cheese

¼ teaspoon salt
Pepper
⅛ teaspoon ground thyme

Dredge zucchini lightly in flour. Heat olive oil in skillet and cook zucchini in it until crisp. Combine eggs, Parmesan, salt, pepper and thyme. Pour over zucchini. Cook until well set on both sides, turning over once.

Baked Spinach Omelet

(FRITTATA DI SPINACI AL FORNO)

3 pounds fresh spinach	⅛ teaspoon nutmeg (optional)
2 tablespoons butter	6 eggs
½ teaspoon salt	¼ cup grated Parmesan cheese
Pepper	

With kitchen scissors, cut spinach leaves into shreds; remove coarse stalks and roots. (This saves chopping the spinach later.) Wash spinach well. Place in deep saucepan. Cook, covered, without additional water, over medium heat for 3 to 5 minutes, or until just tender. Drain thoroughly in strainer and squeeze dry with spoon or hands. Return spinach to the saucepan. Add butter, salt, pepper and nutmeg. Cook over high heat, stirring constantly, until butter is melted and coats spinach. Beat together eggs and Parmesan cheese. Grease a deep 8-inch layer pan or square baking pan with salad oil on bottom and all sides. Place pan on low heat. Pour in half of egg mixture. Cook, like an omelet, until set. Remove from heat. Spread spinach evenly on top of omelet. Pour remaining egg over spinach. Bake in preheated moderate oven (350° F.) for 20 to 25 minutes or until set. Unmold on hot plate. Serve with sautéed mushroom caps or with mushroom sauce.

Potato and Cheese Tart

(TORTINO DI PATATE)

This recipe yields a savory, though substantial, dish.

3 medium-size potatoes, boiled
* and mashed*
1 cup flour
Salt
Pepper
Scant ½ cup olive oil

1 cup canned tomatoes, drained
½ pound mozzarella cheese,
* diced*
¼ cup grated Parmesan cheese
1 tablespoon rosemary

Work together thoroughly mashed potatoes, flour, and salt and pepper to taste. In large shallow oiled baking dish arrange potato mixture in a layer that is about ½ inch thick. Sprinkle with half the olive oil. Top with tomatoes, mozzarella and Parmesan cheese and rosemary. Sprinkle with remaining olive oil. Bake in preheated hot (400° F.) oven 20 to 25 minutes, or until the cheese is light brown. Serve hot, as an entree or with cold meats.

Mozzarella Skewers

(CROSTINI ALLA MOZZARELLA)

The original mozzarella came from around Naples, where in some swamps there used to be herds of buffalo, whose milk went into cheese making. American mozzarella is much blander and more rubberlike than real Italian mozzarella; nevertheless, these crostini are good. It is essential that they be served with the anchovy butter.

Remove the crust from a loaf of French or Italian bread. Cut loaf into slices about ⅓ inch thick. Cut mozzarella in the same size and thickness as bread. Place alternate slices of bread and cheese on a skewer until there are 3 layers of cheese, beginning and ending with bread. Preheat baking dish and place skewers on it. Bake in a preheated, very hot (450° to 475° F.) oven, and bake just long enough for the cheese to melt and the bread to brown.

Melt ½ pound butter. Chop 8 anchovy fillets and simmer in butter for 5 minutes. Pour some of this anchovy butter over each skewer. Serve as hot as you can.

Eggs with Mushrooms
(UOVA AI FUNGHI)

A good luncheon dish.

FOR TWO:

2 tablespoons butter	*2 slices ham*
¼ pound mushrooms, sliced	*4 eggs*
1 tablespoon brandy	*Salt*
1 tablespoon flour	*Pepper*
⅓ cup hot consommé	*1 tablespoon minced parsley*

In a small saucepan, heat 1 tablespoon of the butter. Cook mushrooms in it, stirring constantly, for about 3 minutes. Sprinkle with brandy. Stir in flour. Add consommé. Cook, stirring frequently, for about 5 minutes. (The sauce should be rather thick.) While mushrooms are cooking, heat remaining butter in a skillet. Add ham to it, placing slices side by side. Cook until golden, turning once. Lower heat. Break eggs over ham, two on each slice. Top with mushroom sauce and salt and pepper to taste. Cover tightly. Cook over low heat until eggs are set. Sprinkle with parsley. Serve with slices of toasted dark bread.

Fondue from the Piedmont
(LA FONDUA PIEMONTESE)

This classic dish is quite different from the true Swiss fondue.
The proper cheese for it is Fontina, a buttery cheese from
Piedmont that melts easily; it can be bought in Italian grocery
stores and specialty cheese shops. The glory of a proper Fondua
is the incomparably aromatic white truffles from Alba, which
many people consider superior to black truffles. They too can
sometimes be found fresh in Italian groceries, or canned in
gourmet shops. The combination of cheese and white truffles
is truly out of this world. Short of Fontina cheese, the dish may
be made with Swiss or Gruyère cheese.

1½ to 2 pounds Fontina cheese	*Salt*
Milk	*Pepper*
2 tablespoons butter	*Crustless hot buttered toast*
4 egg yolks	*Raw white truffles*

Cut Fontina into very thin slices or small dice. Put into a deep,
narrow container and add milk to cover. Let steep at least for
4 hours. Melt, but do not brown, butter in top of double
boiler. Add beaten egg yolks, cheese, the milk in which the
cheese was steeped, salt and pepper. Cook over low heat, over
simmering, *not* boiling, water, stirring constantly, until cheese,
eggs and milk have formed a thick, smooth cream. There must
be no stringiness to this cream. Put slices of hot buttered
toast into each individual plate. Pour Fondua over toast, and
cover each helping with very thinly sliced raw white truffles.
Serve immediately.

FISH AND SEA FOOD

FISH AND SEA FOOD of all kinds are an important part of the Italian diet and, along the seacoast which surrounds the country on three sides, a major source of animal proteins. Fish and sea food are far less expensive than meat, since no expense is involved in their raising as it is with meat animals, and they can also be caught for free. An enormous variety of fish, molluscs and crustaceans inhabit the Italian seas, but very few of these colorful and tasty products of the sea can be found in our waters. Thus I have omitted the ways in which to serve the ricci (sea urchins), vongole (a kind of clam), polipi (cuttle-fish and octopus) and so on, and I have also gone easy on other fish recipes. The reason for this is that Italian fish cookery is simple, not at all like French cookery, relying on the flavor of the fish for variety.

Fish soups, composed of a number of different fish and

seasonings, are found all along the Italian coastline. Their variety, too, stems from the different fish that are found in the various localities.

The crustacean that Italian restaurants call scampi in America, when they really mean shrimp, is not a shrimp as we know it, but a kind of prawn or langoustine and closer to the lobster than to shrimp.

Deep-Fried Fish Fillets, Italian Style
(PESCE FRITTO)

The fact that the fish is fried in olive oil rather than shortening is responsible for the different flavor and crisp texture of this fried fish. Small fish are also fried this way. It is the most popular Italian way of cooking fish.

4 medium fillets	*Salt*
½ cup flour	*Lemon wedges*
1 cup olive oil or more	

Coat fillets in flour. Fry in hot olive oil for about 8 minutes on each side. Drain on paper towels. Sprinkle with salt and serve with lemon wedges.

Little Fish, Neapolitan Style
(PESCIOLINI ALLA NAPOLETANA)

Split, bone, and wash small fish such as smelts. Oil a round baking dish and arrange fish in several circles, heads all facing the same way. Pour about ¼ inch of French dressing (made from two-thirds oil and one-third lemon juice—do not use vinegar) over fish. Sprinkle a few fresh or dried herbs, such as thyme, basil or oregano, over fish. Cover and bake in pre-heated hot (425° F.) oven about 10 minutes, depending on size of fish. Test with toothpick for doneness. Do not overbake.

Fish in Wine Sauce

(PESCE AL VINO BIANCO)

Bass, sea bass, perch, trout, swordfish, any non-oily fish is good cooked in this manner. Large fish should be cut into fillets. Small fish, cleaned and split, may be left whole.

2 pounds fish	*2 minced anchovies (optional)*
Salt	*2 tablespoons minced parsley*
Pepper	*1 cup dry white wine*
Flour for dredging	*About ⅓ cup fish stock or*
½ cup olive oil	*chicken bouillon*
1 tablespoon minced onion	*Lemon wedges*

If the fish is large, cut it into 3- to 4-inch pieces. Season lightly with salt and pepper. Dredge lightly with flour and shake off excess flour. Heat half of the olive oil in a skillet. Sauté fish in hot oil, turning over once, until browned and cooked through. Cooking time depends on the kind and thickness of the fish; it should flake at the touch of a fork. Do not overcook.

Drain, place on deep serving dish and keep hot. While fish is cooking, heat remaining olive oil in a saucepan. Add onion, anchovies, parsley and wine to it. Cook over medium heat, stirring constantly, until onion is soft and the sauce reduced to about ⅔ cup. Add fish stock and simmer for about 3 minutes. Correct seasonings. Pour sauce over fish. Serve with boiled new potatoes, with lemon wedges as garnish.

Note: This sauce is also good on fried chicken, cut into bite-size pieces.

Baked Fish with Green Sauce
(PESCE AL FORNO AL VERDE)

Any white fillets of fish, or medium white fish, cleaned and split, may be used for this dish.

2 pounds fish	*Juice of ½ lemon*
Salt	*About ⅓ cup fine dry bread*
Pepper	*crumbs*
⅓ cup minced parsley	*½ cup olive oil*
2 tablespoons minced chives or	
spring onions	

Spread fish in oiled shallow baking dish. Season lightly with salt and pepper. Sprinkle parsley, chives and lemon juice over fish. Top with a thin layer of bread crumbs. Drizzle olive oil over everything. Bake, uncovered, in preheated moderate oven (375° F.) for 20 to 25 minutes, or until fish flakes and top is crisp. Serve hot or cold with lemon wedges.

Trout Cooked in White Wine
(TROTE IN BIANCO)

Any delicate fish or fillets can be cooked this way.

2 cups water	*1 3-inch piece of celery*
2 cups dry white wine	*1 sprig parsley*
1 teaspoon salt	*2 slices lemon*
2 peppercorns	*¼ cup olive oil*
1 bay leaf	*4½-pound trout or 2 or 3 larger*
1 small onion, sliced	*trout*
½ small carrot	

Combine all ingredients except trout. Simmer, covered, for 30 minutes. Strain. Bring liquid to a gentle boil again. Place trout in liquid. Simmer, covered, over lowest possible heat, without boiling, for 10 to 15 minutes, depending on the size of the fish. Remove fish to a hot platter. Serve with green sauce, see page 167. Makes 4 servings.

Fresh Tuna with Peas

(TONNO CON PISELLI)

Fresh tuna is delicious and greatly prized in Italy. Since many American sports fishermen catch it, and do not know how to cook it, I offer this Italian favorite.

6 tablespoons olive oil	Salt
½ medium onion, minced	Pepper
1 tablespoon tomato paste	Flour for dredging
⅔ cup hot water	½ cup dry white wine
¼ cup minced parsley	2 pounds fresh tuna, cut into
2 pounds fresh peas, shelled or	½- to 1-inch slices
2 10-ounce packages frozen	
peas, thawed	

In heavy saucepan, heat 3 tablespoons of the olive oil. Cook onion in it, stirring constantly, until soft. Do not brown. Stir in tomato paste and hot water. Cook 2 minutes. Add parsley and peas. Season with salt and pepper. Simmer, covered, over low heat until peas are half cooked. Stir occasionally. While peas are cooking, heat remaining oil in large, deep, heavy skillet. Dredge tuna slices in flour. Brown on both sides in hot oil. Add wine and cook 3 minutes. Pour peas and sauce over tuna slices. Cook, covered, over medium heat for 10 to 12 minutes, or until fish flakes when pierced with a fork. Cooking time depends on thickness of fish slices. Serve with lemon wedges and boiled new parsleyed potatoes.

Garlic-Broiled Shrimp

(SCAMPI AL FERRI)

2 pounds raw shrimp
2 garlic cloves, minced
½ to ⅔ cup olive oil
2 teaspoons salt

⅓ cup chopped parsley
Juice of 2 lemons
Lemon wedges

Split shrimp shells with scissors. Remove shells. Using a sharp pointed knife, devein shrimps. Arrange shrimps in shallow baking pan. Sprinkle with garlic, olive oil, salt and half of parsley. Broil about 4 inches from source of heat for about 5 to 7 minutes on each side, depending on size of shrimp. Sprinkle with remaining parsley and lemon juice. Serve with lemon wedges.

Fried Squid

(CALAMARETTI FRITTI)

Very popular in Rome and on the whole Italian seacoast, especially in the southern parts of the country. Squid is not a handsome critter, though, when cooked properly, it will be tender and delicate. The following recipe has the virtue of being tasty and making the squid look neutral.

2 pounds small squid
Flour
Salt

1 cup olive oil
Lemon wedges

Have the squid cleaned, skinned and its insides removed. Or see below. Wash and dry. Cut the body into ¼-inch rings and the tentacles into strips. Dip into flour seasoned with salt. Fry in hot olive oil until crisp and browned. Drain. Serve hot with lemon wedges.

HOW TO CLEAN SQUID

(It is quite quickly and easily done): Have ready a good-sized bowl filled with lukewarm water. Working *in* the water, remove the insides from the pocket-like part of the fish. Pull out the spine bone. Remove the purple outside skin. Remove the ink bag from each side of the head, as well as the eyes and the hard core in the center of the tentacles. Rinse the fish under running water until free of all sand and grit. The cleaned fish should be milky white.

Conch, Neapolitan Fashion

(SCUNGILLI ALLA MARINARA)

The pulp of the conch is a favorite Neapolitan dish.

1½ to 2 pounds scungilli pulp, thinly sliced
¼ cup olive oil
1 clove garlic or more to taste
1 small onion, diced
1 medium stalk celery, diced
1½ cups canned tomatoes
½ cup dry white wine
1 tablespoon tomato paste diluted with 2 tablespoons water
½ teaspoon salt
½ teaspoon dried oregano
¼ teaspoon dried basil
1 bay leaf
¼ teaspoon hot pepper seeds or to taste

Boil scungilli in water to cover for about 15 minutes; drain. In deep skillet, heat olive oil. Add scungilli and all other ingredients. Simmer, covered, over low heat until scungilli is tender. Stir frequently. Serve hot, with a green vegetable. Or serve as a sauce over pasta.

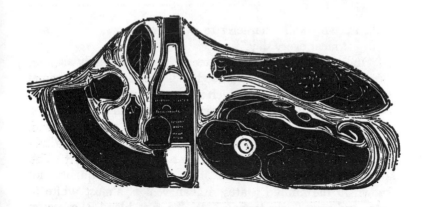

MEAT AND FOWL

To an American used to eating meat two and even three times a day it will come as a surprise that many millions of Italians eat meat perhaps once a week, and yet manage to do a great deal of hard manual work. Meat has always been a luxury in Italy, where pasture, compared to the country's size, is scarce and the investment that a cow represents beyond the means of the majority of the peasants, especially in the South. Though there are many recipes for big cuts of beef, lamb, veal and kid, there are far more for small cuts, such as stews and the family of cutlets, scaloppine, fettine, etc., which represent the bulk of Italian meat cookery—short-order cookery, I would say. No other cuisine has so perfected the art of making a tiny slice of veal delicious in as many ways as the Italian one.

A roast, commonplace to Americans, is a treat to most

Italians, who still characterize worldly success by saying, "they eat meat every day."

Italian beef, with certain exceptions, is not nearly as good as American beef. The only good beef comes from the animal called vitellone, big veal, which is not veal in the Italian sense, but an animal generally between six months and three years, which has never been made to work like cows and oxen. Veal, or vitello, is the flesh of a calf that has never fed on anything but its mother's milk, and which has been slaughtered when a few weeks or months old. It is of a superb quality not known in the United States; Italian veal is almost white in color and very finely textured. Its flavor is bland, the reason why the Italian veal dishes call for the savory touches of herbs, prosciutto and wines. Italian lamb is also far more delicate than ours. Kid, the young of the goat, is a favorite meat in Rome and farther south, and it can be utterly delicious. The pork is equally good. Generally speaking, the meat in Northern Italy is infinitely superior to that of the South, where it tends to be tough and stringy.

Until the fairly recent advent of broiler factory-produced chickens, a chicken was also in the treat category. Today, and justly so, a distinction is made between the factory-produced fowl and the, so to speak, home-grown ones. The latter are infinitely tastier, and also more expensive. Duck has never been widely used, except for the wild ducks and, of course, those raised in the farmer's yard. Turkeys, too, are the exception rather than the rule.

Italians are passionate hunters, and in some parts of the country there still is some wild game like hare and boar to be found, though no deer, or practically none. Immensely popular are the small, wild songbirds like larks, which are shot down pitilessly. The sight of their tiny bodies in the shops is indeed a sad one; however delicious they may be, it does not seem right to kill them.

Savory herbs are used a good deal in Italian meat

cookery, and tomatoes with a very light hand. The wine used is white, rather than red, and, because of its more intensive flavor, Marsala is more common than either.

In Italy, a meat dish is not inevitably accompanied by potatoes or another starch. Quite the contrary; its contorno, or what goes around it, is usually a vegetable or a salad, the starchy part of the meal being the soup, spaghetti or other pasta, rice, polenta or dumplings that preceded the meat. The one exception is the Milanese specialty of Ossobuco, veal shanks, which is served with saffron rice.

Until recently, fowl of any kind was a luxury in Italy and was served in the home only to very honored guests and upon special occasions. Chickens, capons (the Italians are extremely fond of them) and turkeys were hand raised by the peasant women, with more or less care. On the whole, these animals were rather thin, and muscular from a healthy outdoor life. It was not unusual for particular housewives, such as my mother, to have an arrangement with a peasant wife about chickens, so that they would be plump and tender, especially raised for her. Now, commercial chicken raising is on the rise, and frozen chickens are even imported from the United States. Italian gourmets claim that these are not nearly as tasty as the ones fed by hand and with grain only, and there are constant discussions on the subject. Restaurants will advertise their special grain-fed animals as a come-on.

Because of the past poor quality of chickens, capons were greatly prized, and a stuffed capon served as an extremely fancy dish at many a Christmas or a wedding, especially in Southern Italy. The stuffings were on the heavy and spiced side, with sausages, herbs and the like, and for my taste, too much of a muchness.

Turkey has never caught the Italian imagination as it has the American one. When it does appear, it will be served stuffed, and more often in Northern Italy than anywhere else; or turkey breasts are sautéed in butter as a great treat.

Fried Steaks

(FETTINE IN PADELLA)

Thin little steaks, such as shell steaks, boneless sirloin—in fact, any tender beef sliced small and very thin—are standard Italian family eating. These resemble in no way an American steak. The cooking is of the simplest and quickest.

Have your beef thinly sliced and trimmed free of all fat. Heat a very little olive oil in a skillet. Over medium heat, cook steaks in it very quickly—2 to 3 minutes on each side. Season with salt and pepper to taste. Serve with lemon wedges.

Note: Sometimes the steaks are dipped in a little flour and the pan gravy thinned with a drop of wine and poured over the cooked meat.

Florentine Steaks

(LA BISTECCA ALLA FIORENTINA)

This is a famous dish, since Tuscany is renowned for the excellence of its beef. The true Florentine steak should come from an animal that is no more than two years old; it is a porterhouse, sirloin or any other tender steak. Meat is a luxury in Italy to this day, and usually used in small quantities, so that one of the delights of the Bistecca alla Fiorentina is its size and thickness. It should be the size of a plate and about 1½ inches thick, which is unusual in Italy.

Like all steaks, the Florentine variety has inspired various schools of thought. One says that the steak should be simply broiled over a very hot charcoal fire for 5 to 7 minutes on each side, and served plain, with perhaps a little butter on it after it is cooked. Another school—and this is the one I subscribe to—rubs the steak with a cut garlic clove, a little pepper and a tablespoon or two of good olive oil, letting it stand at room temperature for an hour or two before cooking, so that there will be no trace of the refrigerator's chill. Yet a third school cooks the steak plainly, but deposits the finished meat on a dish with a little excellent olive oil on it, coating it on both sides.

In any case, the steak should be well browned on the outside, and rare to medium inside. It is salted when almost done, and served with lemon wedges.

If a gas or electric broiler is used, it should be preheated at the highest temperature for at least 10 minutes.

Sicilian Beef Ragout with Onions
(STUFATO ALLA SICILIANA)

Aromatic and spicy, like all good Sicilian cooking.

1 tablespoon butter
5 tablespoons olive oil
3 pounds top round of beef, cut into 2-inch pieces
1 cup dry red wine
2 cups Italian-style canned tomatoes
2 tablespoons tomato paste

3 pounds small white onions, whole
2 cloves garlic
2-inch piece whole cinnamon
4 whole cloves
1 bay leaf
Salt
Pepper
Chopped parsley

Heat butter and 2 tablespoons of the olive oil in heavy casserole or Dutch oven and brown meat on all sides. Add ½ cup of the wine, cover, and simmer for 10 minutes. Add tomatoes and tomato paste and continue to simmer, covered. Heat remaining oil in skillet and very quickly brown onions in it. Add onions to meat, together with garlic, cinnamon, cloves, bay leaf and remaining wine. Season to taste. Cover pan and simmer extremely slowly for about 3 hours, or until meat is tender and the sauce the consistency of purée. Stir occasionally, and add a little water if needed. Sprinkle with parsley and serve with Rice Pilaf.

Roman Meatballs

(POLPETTINE ALLA ROMANA)

These meatballs should be finely textured. This is achieved by thoroughly working together the ingredients; a Roman cook would do it with her hands, tossing the mixture to and fro. In Italy meatballs are *never* served with spaghetti; this is an American custom.

4 slices firm white bread
½ cup water
½ pound ground beef
½ pound lean pork, ground
½ pound ground veal
1 medium onion, grated or very
*   finely minced*
1 clove garlic, very finely
*   minced*
1 cup minced parsley
Grated rind of 1 lemon

2 eggs
2 tablespoons pignoli nuts,
*   chopped (optional)*
2 tablespoons grated Parmesan
*   cheese*
½ teaspoon salt
¼ teaspoon pepper
⅛ teaspoon nutmeg
Fine dry bread crumbs
Olive oil or lard for sautéing

Trim bread free of crusts. Crumble and soak in water for about 5 minutes. Squeeze dry. In a deep bowl, combine all ingredients except bread crumbs and olive oil. Mix thoroughly. Let stand for 1 hour. Shape mixture into about 12 to 15 meatballs. Coat each meatball in bread crumbs. In a large skillet, heat oil or lard to the depth of 1 inch. Over medium heat, brown meatballs in it on all sides. Lower heat and cook about 15 minutes, shaking skillet frequently to prevent sticking. Drain on absorbent paper. Serve hot with a tomato or green sauce, potatoes and a green vegetable.

Mother's Roman Meatloaf

(IL POLPETTONE ROMANO DI MAMMÀ)

There are many kinds of Italian meatloaves, but I think my mother's savory version is one of the best. Italian meatloaves have a fine-grained, solid texture, which is achieved by kneading all ingredients with the hands, and tossing the mixture from one hand to the other, like a ball. Incidentally, Italians do not consider meatloaf a poor man's dish, as Americans do, but as a good thing, fit for parties.

2 pounds ground beef
½ pound ground veal
½ pound ground pork
1 teaspoon salt
½ teaspoon pepper
2 teaspoons dried basil
½ cup grated Parmesan cheese
½ cup fine dried breadcrumbs

¼ cup minced onion
¼ cup minced parsley
1 garlic clove, minced
1 tablespoon grated lemon rind
3 eggs, beaten
3 shelled hard-cooked eggs
1 cup consommé

In deep bowl, combine all ingredients except hard-cooked eggs and consommé. Mix thoroughly with hands. On waxed paper, pat out mixture into a 10-by-12-inch rectangle. Place hard-cooked eggs lengthwise on meat. Roll up into a meatloaf. Or divide mixture into 3 parts, making 3 small meatloaves with 1 hard-cooked egg in each. Line a baking pan with aluminum foil. Grease foil. Bake in preheated hot oven (425° F.) for 10 minutes. Lower heat to moderate (350° F.). Add consommé. Bake for 1 hour and 15 minutes or until baked through. Decrease baking time to 45 minutes for small meatloaves. Baste frequently; if necessary, use a little more hot consommé for basting. Transfer meatloaf to hot serving platter. Let stand for 10 minutes to settle the juices and for easier carving. Serve hot or cold.

ELEGANT VARIATION

Omit stuffing meatloaf with the 3 hard-cooked eggs. In their stead, spread meat with about 10 slices of boiled ham or Italian prosciutto. Make a firm omelet with 3 eggs. Top ham slices with omelet. Roll up into a loaf and proceed as directed.

Sardinian Pot Roast

(IL MANZO DI ORISTANO)

As cooked by my mother's nurse, a woman from a Sardinian village near Oristano. The sauce is deliciously aromatic.

1 ounce imported dried mushrooms (2½-ounce packages, chopped)	*½ teaspoon ground marjoram*
	1 bay leaf
	2 cloves
⅔ cup water	*1 teaspoon salt*
2 cups chopped parsley	*½ teaspoon pepper*
2 garlic cloves, chopped	*1 cup dry white wine*
1 onion, sliced	*3 pounds beef chuck or bottom*
1 teaspoon dried rosemary,	*eye of round*
crumbled	*1 tablespoon lard*

Soak dried mushrooms in water. In deep bowl (do not use aluminum) combine parsley, garlic cloves, onion, rosemary, marjoram, bay leaf, cloves, salt, pepper and wine. Add mushrooms and their liquid. Mix well. Trim meat of all fat. Place meat in marinade, coating it on all sides. Let stand in marinade for 2 to 4 hours. Remove meat from marinade; reserve marinade. Dry meat on kitchen toweling. Heat lard in a deep saucepan or casserole that will just hold the meat. Brown meat on all sides in hot lard. Pour marinade over meat. Simmer, covered, turning occasionally, for 1½ to 2 hours or until meat is tender. Slice meat and place on deep heated platter. Keep warm. Strain pot liquid through fine strainer, or, better still, purée in blender. The sauce should be the consistency of a thin mayonnaise. Heat sauce and pour over sliced meat. Serve with boiled new potatoes and a green vegetable.

Chicken and Veal Roll

(POLPETTONE DI POLLO E VITELLO)

A good dish for a party or a picnic. There should be equal quantities of boneless chicken and veal, that is, about one pound each.

1 pound veal
2 large chicken legs and 1 large chicken breast
½ pound sausage meat
2 eggs, beaten
⅓ cup flour
¾ cup grated Parmesan cheese
⅓ cup chopped pistachio nuts
2 tablespoons dry Marsala or brandy
Salt
Pepper
⅛ teaspoon nutmeg
About 1 quart chicken bouillon
1 cup dry white wine

Trim veal free of all fat and gristle. Take skin off chicken pieces. With a sharp knife, cut all meat off the bones; discard the bones. Put veal and chicken through the fine blade of a meat grinder twice. The second time, add sausage meat. Put mixture into a bowl and mix thoroughly with hands or a wooden spoon. Blending well after each addition, add eggs, flour, Parmesan cheese, pistachios, nutmeg and Marsala. Season lightly with salt and pepper.

On lightly floured board, spread mixture into a rectangle about 8 inches by 12 inches. (A floured rolling pin is helpful.) Roll up as in a jelly roll. Pat firm and smooth into the shape of a sausage. Take 4 thicknesses of cheesecloth or a piece of clean linen. Cut it into a piece that will be large enough to wrap around the meat roll. Allow an overlap of 2 inches at either side which will serve as handles. Spread cloth generously with butter. Place meat roll on it. Roll up tightly; the roll should be smooth and even. Tie at both ends, leaving 2 handles for lifting the roll. Place roll into a kettle large enough to hold it comfortably. Add bouillon to cover. Cover and bring to a boil. Reduce heat to lowest possible and add wine. Simmer, covered, for about 1½ hours. Lift out by handles. Drain and reserve broth for soup. Cool meat roll between two plates in cool place or in refrigerator. Put a weight on the top plate (heavy can, electric iron, etc.) to press meat down. After 4 hours, remove from cloth. Wrap in aluminum foil until serving time. Cut into thin slices. Serve with other cold cuts, such as tongue, with pickles and a salad. Makes 8 to 10 servings.

Note: If used as an appetizer, the roll may also be glazed with a clear aspic or served with a herb-lemon mayonnaise.

Saltimbocca

A Roman specialty which means, literally, they jump into your mouth.

2 pounds veal scaloppine, each piece about 5 inches square
1 teaspoon dried sage
¼ pound prosciutto or ham, sliced thin

3 tablespoons butter
Salt
Pepper
2 to 3 tablespoons dry white wine

Sprinkle veal slices with sage and place equal-size slices of ham on them. Pin them together with toothpicks. Melt butter and fry meat in it. Season to taste. Cook, covered, over high heat for 2 to 3 minutes on each side until veal is browned. Place slices of cooked meat on heated platter, ham side up. Keep hot. Add wine to pan and scrape bottom. Boil up once. Pour sauce over meat and serve hot.

Scaloppine al Marsala

This is about the same dish as Saltimbocca, except that no ham is used and it is made with Marsala instead of white wine.

Bocconcini

Another variation. A thin slice of Swiss cheese is substituted for the ham.

Veal Uccelletto from Liguria
(VITELLO ALL'UCCELLETTO)

This dish should have a pronounced flavor of bay leaf.

1½ pounds veal scaloppine	⅓ cup dry white wine or
¼ cup olive oil	consommé
1 garlic clove	Salt
3 or 4 bay leaves	Pepper

Cut the veal into 2- to 3-inch pieces. Heat olive oil. Add veal, garlic clove and bay leaves. Cook over medium heat, stirring constantly, until veal is golden brown. Add wine, salt and pepper to taste. Cook for 5 to 7 more minutes.

Note: Peas are a standard accompaniment to this dish. They may be cooked separately, or added to the meat with the wine or broth. Two cups of tender young peas would be sufficient.

Veal Lucullus from Piedmont

(VITELLO LUCULLO ALLA PIEMONTESE)

To be perfectly correct, the cheese used should be Fontina, a semisoft cheese from Piedmont. But since this is seldom found in America, substitutes must be used in this rather elegant dish. For each person:

1 veal chop, cut 1 inch thick	*1 thin slice Swiss or Muenster*
Salt	*cheese*
Pepper	*1 slice black or white truffle*
1 thin slice prosciutto or ham	*Butter*
	Dry white wine

Have butcher cut a pocket in each chop. Sprinkle with salt and pepper. Insert ham, cheese, and truffle in each chop. Fasten tightly with toothpicks. Brown on both sides in butter. Pour off excess butter. Add enough wine to come three quarters of the way to top of chops. Cover pan tightly and simmer about 15 minutes, or until chops are tender. Remove to hot platter and keep hot. Boil up sauce to reduce it and pour over chops. Serve very hot, and, if you want to be really Italian, with a French-dressed green salad.

Veal Cutlets with Mushrooms and Peppers
(COTOLETTE DI VITELLO CON FUNGHI E PEPERONI)

The sweet red or yellow bell peppers make for a more decorative dish, but any green peppers may be used.

2 peppers	Salt
5 tablespoons olive oil	Pepper
½ pound mushrooms, sliced	⅛ teaspoon oregano
1 pound thin veal cutlets	1½ to 2 cups canned Italian tomatoes

Place peppers over high heat, directly on the burners, and roast until outer skin is black and blistered. Using your fingers, peel off outer skin under running cold water. This method may be hot on your fingers, but the cold water will cool them. Trim peppers free of membrane and seeds. Dry well between paper toweling. Cut peppers into ¾-inch squares or strips. Heat half of the oil in heavy saucepan or casserole. Add peppers and cook over medium heat, stirring constantly, for 2 minutes. Add mushrooms and cook for 2 more minutes. Add tomatoes, salt, pepper and oregano. Cook, covered, over low heat for 15 minutes, stirring occasionally. Heat remaining olive oil in skillet. Brown veal cutlets in it on both sides. Add veal to tomato sauce. Simmer, covered, about 10 to 15 minutes longer, depending on the thickness of the veal cutlets. Stir occasionally. If sauce is too thick, add a little hot water, a tablespoon at a time. If too thin, cook, uncovered, until the right consistency. Serve with home-fried potatoes followed by a tossed green salad.

Veal Cutlets with Artichokes

(FETTE DI VITELLO CON CARCIOFI)

6 boneless veal cutlets
Flour for dredging
6 tablespoons butter
2 tablespoons olive oil
½ cup canned bouillon
3 medium artichokes, trimmed
     and very thinly sliced and
     dry

½ cup dry white wine
Salt
Pepper
⅓ cup minced parsley
Juice of ½ lemon
1 lemon, sliced
Parsley sprigs

With a meat mallet, rolling pin or beer bottle, pound cutlets until very thin. Trim into even sizes. Dredge cutlets in flour; shake off excess flour. Using 2 large skillets, put 3 tablespoons butter and 1 tablespoon olive oil in each. Heat butter and oil in one skillet and add the cutlets. Brown on both sides over medium to high heat. Add bouillon and simmer over low heat 4 to 8 minutes, depending on the thickness of the cutlets, or until done. While cutlets are cooking, heat butter and oil in the second skillet. Add artichoke slices (prepared as described on pages 143–144) and wine. Cook over medium heat, shaking pan frequently, for 5 minutes or until tender. Turn occasionally with spatula to prevent sticking and browning. Season meat and artichokes lightly with salt and pepper to taste. Remove cutlets to heated platter and spread the artichoke slices over them. Keep warm. Combine juices from both skillets in one. Add parsley and lemon juice and bring to a quick boil. Pour sauce over veal and artichokes. Garnish with lemon slices and parsley sprigs. Serve immediately, with small boiled new potatoes.

Veal Cutlets Parmesan

(COTOLETTE DI VITELLO ALLA PARMIGIANA)

1 pound veal cutlets	½ cup grated Parmesan cheese
2 eggs, beaten	½ cup olive oil
Salt	1½ to 2 cups canned Italian
Pepper	tomatoes
1 cup fine dry bread crumbs	½ pound mozzarella cheese, sliced

Trim cutlets to even size and remove all gristle. Combine eggs
with a little salt and pepper. (Do not oversalt since the cheeses
are salty.) Dip cutlets into beaten eggs. Shake off excess moisture. Combine bread crumbs and Parmesan cheese. Coat cutlets
with mixture on all sides and shake off excess. Heat olive oil in
large skillet. Brown cutlets in it on both sides. Depending on
the thickness of the cutlets, this will take 5 to 8 minutes. Place
cutlets in greased shallow 1½-quart baking dish. Top with
canned tomatoes. Cover with mozzarella slices. Bake in preheated moderate oven (350° F.) for about 10 to 15 minutes, or
until mozzarella is melted and golden. Serve with buttered
green beans that have, if desired, been sprinkled with a little
lemon juice.

Maria Anghileri's Veal Roast

(L'ARROSTO DI VITELLO DI MARIA ANGHILERI)

A juicy roast of veal, cooked in its own juice. The flavor trick
is not to sear the meat first, but to combine all the *cold* ingredients. There must not be one trace of fat on the veal and it
should be cooked in a tightly closed saucepan or casserole just
big enough to hold it.

3 *pounds boneless rolled
    shoulder of veal, without
    any fat*
Salt
Pepper

½ *teaspoon ground sage*
2 *tablespoons butter*
2 *tablespoons olive oil*
¼ *cup cold water*

Rub meat on all sides with salt, pepper and sage. In a heavy saucepan or casserole, combine meat, butter and olive oil. Heat slowly. Cook over medium heat, turning several times, until the meat is reddish on all sides. Sprinkle with cold water. Lower heat to lowest possible. Simmer, tightly covered, for about 1½ hours or until meat is done; cooking time depends on the age and tenderness of the veal. Check occasionally for moisture; if necessary, add a little more cold water, one tablespoon at a time, to prevent sticking. At the end of the cooking time, there should be about ½ to ⅔ cup pan gravy. Carve veal and pour pan gravy over it.

Old-Fashioned Veal Stew
(STUFATINO DI VITELLO ALL'ANTICA)

2 *tablespoons olive oil*
1½ *pounds boneless veal, cut
    into 1-inch cubes*
1 *tablespoon butter*
¼ *cup minced prosciutto or
    lean bacon*
¼ *cup minced parsley*
½ *garlic clove, minced*
½ *medium onion, minced*
1 *leek, sliced, green and white
    parts*

1 *stalk celery, chopped*
3 *tomatoes, peeled, seeded and
    chopped*
1 *sliced carrot*
1 *artichoke, thinly sliced*
½ *cup dry white wine*
½ *cup bouillon*
Salt
Pepper

Heat olive oil in a skillet. Over high heat, brown veal in it. (The heat must be high, or the veal will stew rather than sear, and lose its juices.) In a casserole or deep saucepan, combine butter, prosciutto, parsley, garlic and onion. Cook over medium heat, stirring constantly, for 3 minutes. Add veal and all other ingredients. (The artichoke should be prepared as described on pages 143–144.) Simmer, covered, over low heat for 25 minutes or until veal is tender. Check for moisture; if necessary, add a little more bouillon. Serve with boiled potatoes.

Note: A handful of peas may be added to the stew, or mushrooms, with or in lieu of the artichoke.

Florentine Broiled Breast of Veal

(PETTO DI VITELLO ALLA GRATELLA)

3 *to 4 pounds breast of veal*	¼ *cup olive oil*
Boiling water	3 *tablespoons lemon juice*
2 *teaspoons salt*	*Grated rind of 1 lemon*
3 *whole peppercorns*	2 *tablespoons chopped parsley*
1 *stalk celery*	⅛ *teaspoon nutmeg*
1 *carrot*	1 *tablespoon butter, melted*
1 *onion*	2 *large eggs, beaten*
1 *cup dry white wine*	*Fine dry bread crumbs*

Put breast of veal into deep kettle. Add boiling water to cover, salt, peppercorns, celery, carrot, onion and wine. Simmer, covered, for about 45 minutes or until veal is tender. Remove meat. Strain liquid and use for soups. Remove all bones and gristle from meat. Place meat on large platter. Cover with another large platter and weigh down with canned foods, electric iron or anything heavy. This will flatten the meat.

In a bowl, combine olive oil, lemon juice, lemon rind,

parsley and nutmeg to make a marinade. When meat is cool, cut into 1- to 2-inch strips. Put meat into marinade. Let stand for 2 hours, turning occasionally so that the marinade can penetrate the meat on all sides. Dry meat between kitchen toweling. Combine melted butter and eggs. Dip meat into mixture. Coat with bread crumbs. Place meat strips in one layer on broiler. Broil under medium heat until golden. Turn and broil on other side. Line a warmed serving dish with a napkin and arrange meat on it; this will keep the meat hot. Serve immediately with a tartar or green sauce.

Note: The meat may also be placed in a greased shallow baking dish in one layer and baked in preheated moderate oven (375° F.) for 15 minutes or until golden. Turn and bake for 10 more minutes.

Braised Veal with Lemon

(FILONI DI VITELLO AL LIMONE)

There should be only a little sauce in this dish.

2 pounds boneless veal	*⅔ cup dry white wine*
Flour	*Salt*
3 tablespoons butter	*Pepper*
Juice of 2 large lemons	*⅓ cup minced parsley*

Trim all fat, gristle and membranes from veal. Cut into 1½-inch pieces. Coat with flour; shake off excess flour. Melt butter in heavy saucepan. Over high heat, brown veal in it, stirring constantly. Stir in lemon juice. Reduce heat to lowest possible. Simmer, covered, shaking pan frequently, for 5 minutes. Add wine. Season with salt and pepper. Simmer, covered, for 20 minutes or until veal is tender. Stir frequently. If necessary, to prevent scorching, add a little hot water, a tablespoon at a time. Before serving, sprinkle with parsley. Serve with a green vegetable.

Italian Veal with Tuna Fish

(VITELLO TONNATO)

A summer specialty found everywhere in Italy and a fine buffet dish. Vitello tonnato can be made in any quantity—just increase ingredients proportionately.

2 tablespoons olive oil	2 stalks celery, thinly sliced
3½-pound boneless rolled leg of veal	1 carrot, thinly sliced
	3 sprigs parsley
1 large onion, thinly sliced	½ teaspoon thyme
1 can (2 ounces) anchovy fillets	1 teaspoon salt
	¼ teaspoon freshly ground black pepper
½ sour pickle	
1 can (7 ounces) tuna, drained	4 tablespoons capers
1 cup dry white wine	2 tablespoons lemon juice
2 cloves garlic, cut in halves	Mayonnaise

In a Dutch oven or a deep pot with a tight-fitting cover, heat the oil. Add the meat and brown it very lightly on all sides. Add the onion slices, anchovy fillets, sour pickle, tuna, wine, garlic, celery, carrot, parsley, thyme, salt and pepper. Cover the pot tightly and bring to a boil. Reduce the heat and simmer until the meat is tender, about 2 hours. Remove the meat to a large bowl. Purée the broth over the meat. Place the bowl in the refrigerator and let stand overnight or longer. Just before you are ready to serve it, carve the veal into very thin slices. Arrange the sliced veal on a deep platter. Garnish with capers. Make sauce by blending the marinade (from which fat has been removed) with the lemon juice and enough mayonnaise to give the sauce the consistency of thin cream. Pour sauce over veal slices. Serves 6 to 8.

Italian Veal Roll from Parma

(VITELLO ROLE DI PARMA)

Parma is one of the loveliest Italian cities, home of such specialties (the order of preference is individual) as an imposing twelfth-century cathedral, an incredible octagonal baptistry, the sensuous paintings of Correggio, the home of Verdi, Parma violets, Parmesan cheese, ham, butter and other delicacies. The food is so excellent that people make gastronomic pilgrimages to the town.

1½ pounds veal from leg, trimmed free of fat, sinew and gristle and flattened out as much as possible (ask the butcher to do this)	Pinch of sage
	Pinch of ground cloves
	Enough thin slices of prosciutto ham to cover meat
	2 large or 3 small hard-cooked eggs
Salt	1 tablespoon butter
Pepper	1 tablespoon oil
Grated rind of 1 lemon	½ to ¾ cup dry white wine

Season veal with salt, pepper, lemon rind, sage and cloves. Cover with prosciutto. Place eggs on ham. Roll meat up and tie with string. Melt butter and oil and brown meat roll in it. Pour wine over meat and cover pan tightly. Simmer very slowly for about 2 hours. To serve, cut in slices and serve sauce separately. Veal roll is good cold also; in this case, chill sauce separately until the solid layer of fat can be taken off the top.

Note: This is a pretty dish, the colors of the meats and egg making un'ottima figura (an excellent appearance). I had it in Parma hot, with a dish of Fennel au Gratin. Cold, it would be good with a salad of Belgian endive and with cut-up new potatoes garnished with truffles—which, in Italy, would be white truffles from Piedmont.

Milanese Braised Shin of Veal
(OSSIBUCHI ALLA MILANESE)

A famous dish that shows the typical Italian talent for making do with little meat. There are no tomatoes in it and it should be finished off with gremolata (a mixture of parsley, garlic and chopped lemon peel), or it won't be the traditional Ossibuchi alla Milanese. One shank feeds one person—for more servings, increase proportions accordingly.

2 tablespoons butter
*4 veal shanks, 4 inches long
    and 2 inches thick, with
    plenty of meat (they can
    be ordered from butcher)*
2 tablespoons flour
Salt

Pepper
1 cup dry white wine
Hot bouillon
1 tablespoon minced parsley
1 clove garlic, minced
*Yellow peel of 1 medium-size
    lemon, minced fine*

Heat butter in heavy casserole or Dutch oven. Roll shanks in flour, season with salt and pepper and brown thoroughly, turning several times. Stand shanks upright, so that the marrow in the bones won't fall out as they cook. Pour wine over them and cook uncovered for about 5 minutes. Add ½ cup hot bouillon, cover pan, and cook for about 1 hour, or until tender. Ten minutes before serving, combine parsley, garlic and lemon peel, and place over bones. Cook 5 minutes longer. Check sauce. If too thick, add a little more hot bouillon and a little butter and blend well. If too thin, thicken sauce with about 1 tablespoon butter and ½ tablespoon flour kneaded together into a smooth paste. Risotto alla Milanese is the traditional accompaniment for ossobuchi.

Venetian Liver with Onions
(FEGATO ALLA VENEZIANA)

The best and quickest way to serve liver. The liver slices must be thin or this dish won't come off, since its trick lies in the quick cooking.

1½ pounds calf liver	Salt
¼ cup butter	Pepper
2 tablespoons olive oil	Juice of ½ lemon (or less)
4 large onions, finely chopped	Chopped parsley
¼ cup dry white wine	

Wash and dry liver thoroughly. Cut into very thin strips, 2 inches long. Heat butter and olive oil together in a frying pan and cook onions until soft and golden. Add wine and season to taste. Cook for 2 to 3 minutes. Add liver and fry quickly until brown on both sides. Add lemon juice. Sprinkle with parsley. Serve immediately on a hot platter, with a salad of watercress and Belgian endive dressed with lemon juice and a little oil.

Braised Lamb, Roman Fashion
(ABBACCHIO ALLA ROMANA)

It should be remembered that Italian lamb is far more tender and delicate than ours, since it comes from a milk-fed animal.

For this dish, it is essential to use lard and preferably leaf lard, the fat that is typical of much Roman cooking, and a good deal of pepper.

2 pounds boneless lamb	1/3 cup water
3/4 teaspoon salt	2 tablespoons vinegar
3/4 teaspoon pepper, or to taste	1/2 garlic clove, minced
2 to 3 tablespoons lard	1/2 to 1 teaspoon dried rose-
1 tablespoon flour	mary, crumbled
2/3 cup dry white wine	2 anchovies, minced

Trim lamb of all excess fat and cut into 1½-inch cubes. Sprinkle with salt and pepper. In large, deep skillet, heat lard. Over high heat, brown meat in it on all sides. Sprinkle flour over meat. Add all remaining ingredients. Lower heat to lowest possible. Simmer, covered, stirring occasionally, for about 30 minutes or until meat is tender. If too thick, add a little water, one tablespoon at a time. If too thin, cook, uncovered, to allow for evaporation, until the desired consistency is reached. Serve with boiled or home-fried potatoes.

Lamb Stew with Egg Sauce

(AGNELLO BRODETTATO)

This dish is also made with kid, which is a popular meat in Rome and south of it. I have also used the recipe for veal, in an unorthodox manner, and it comes out very well.

2 pounds boneless lamb or veal	2 tablespoons flour
1/4 cup minced prosciutto or lean bacon	1/2 cup dry white wine
	Hot water
2 tablespoons minced onion	3 egg yolks
1½ tablespoons lard	1½ tablespoons lemon juice
Salt	1/4 cup minced parsley
Pepper	1/2 teaspoon dried marjoram

Trim meat of all excess fat and cut into 1½-inch cubes. In a deep skillet or saucepan, combine lamb, prosciutto, lard and onion. Cook over medium heat, stirring constantly, until lamb is golden—it should not be brown. Season with salt and pepper and sprinkle with flour. Cook 2 minutes longer. Add wine and cook, uncovered, stirring frequently, until the wine has evaporated. Add hot water to almost cover the meat. Simmer, covered, over low heat, stirring frequently, for 35 minutes or until meat is tender. Stir frequently; if necessary, add a little more hot water to prevent scorching. About 10 minutes before serving time, beat together egg yolks, lemon juice, parsley and marjoram. Remove lamb from heat and stir in sauce. Keep in a warm place, but not over direct heat, for about 5 minutes, or until the sauce has set without curdling.

Florentine Pork Roast Arista

A dish that dates back to the Renaissance. Arista, au fond, is a manner of cooking, and I have used it successfully with other roasting cuts of pork, with leg of veal, boned rump of veal and with leg of lamb. Traditionally, pork arista is served cold, but it is also good hot.

Loin of pork, about 3 to 4 pounds
3 cloves garlic, or to taste
1 tablespoon dried rosemary or 2 tablespoons fresh rosemary leaves
3 whole cloves
Salt
Pepper
Red or white dry wine

Trim pork of excess fat. Wet garlic and roll in rosemary. Cut pockets in meat by inserting pointed knife and making each hole large enough to hold a garlic clove. Insert garlic cloves and whole cloves into these pockets, and rub meat with salt and pepper. Place on rack in roasting pan with an equal mixture of water and wine, which should be about 2 inches deep. Cook in open pan in preheated slow (300 °F.) oven. Baste occasionally. Allow 45 minutes' roasting time per pound. Cool in its own juice. The meat should be moist. Serve with cold—not chilled—string beans or broccoli dressed with a simple French dressing. Makes 6 to 8 servings.

Arista Perugina

Proceed as above, but instead of rosemary use fresh fennel leaves, chopped, or fennel seed. A salad of fresh fennel, sliced thin and dressed with oil, salt and pepper only, is an excellent accompaniment.

Cotechino or Zampone from Modena

(COTECHINO O ZAMPONE DI MODENA)

Both Cotechino and Zampone are salami salted for only a few days; they have to be cooked for a long time and are usually eaten hot. These extremely tasty salami are originally specialties from the Emilia and the Romagna, two provinces famous for their excellent food, and especially for their hams and pork dishes. The difference between the two is that the Cotechino looks like a fat, squat salami, whereas the Zampone is stuffed into the skin of a pig's foot. Cotechini and Zamponi, to use the plural, are never made at home, but bought at meat markets and salumerie, or cold-cut specialty shops. They are a winter dish and practically all Italian grocers in the United States carry them. As with all sausages, they may vary slightly in flavor, depending on who makes them, but invariably they are flavorful and rich.

The classic accompaniment for both is a purée of lentils and mashed potatoes, as well as Frutta in Mostarda, that is, pears, figs, apricots, peaches and other fruit preserved in a sweet mustard sauce. Frutta in Mostarda, too, is always bought in the grocery and never made at home. It comes in a sweet and in a sharper version, and all Italian groceries and gourmet markets carry it bottled or canned. It is also an excellent accompaniment for plain boiled, roasted or broiled meats.

To cook Cotechino or Zampone, make a few incisions with a fine skewer or a knitting needle. Place lengthways into a deep kettle. Cover with boiling water. Reduce heat to lowest possible. Simmer, covered, for about 1 hour for each pound of meat. Some of the liquid may be used for making the lentil purée. The remaining liquid can be chilled, degreased and used for soups, since it is very tasty.

To serve, cut Cotechino or Zampone into thick slices. Arrange slices on heated serving platter and surround with lentil purée on one side and mashed potatoes on the other. Serve the Frutta in Mostarda separately.

Hunter's Chicken

(POLLO ALLA CACCIATORE)

There are two versions of this dish—one from Northern and the other from Southern Italy. The latter is a much more powerful dish, containing tomatoes and hot peppers. I prefer the former, since it is more delicate, and rather fragrant.

½ cup butter
1 cup minced onion
½ cup chopped parsley
1 broiler or fryer (2½ to 3 pounds), cut into pieces
1 cup water

1 cup sliced mushrooms
¼ cup minced fresh basil or 1 tablespoon dried basil
1 teaspoon dried rosemary
1 bay leaf
Salt and pepper
½ cup dry white wine

In large skillet, sauté onion in hot butter for 5 minutes, or until soft. Add parsley and cook 1 minute. Add chicken pieces and cook until golden brown. Add water, mushrooms, basil, rosemary, bay leaf, and salt and pepper to taste. Cover and simmer 15 to 20 minutes. Add wine, and cook another 15 to 20 minutes, or until chicken is tender. Serve with buttered noodles.

Note: For a less aromatic dish, reduce quantities of herbs to taste.

Roman Deviled Broiled Chicken

(POLLO ALLA DIAVOLA)

Pollo alla diavola is a classic Roman dish, a recipe that could not be simpler, yet is infinitely more delicious than almost all other broiled chicken. The following recipe serves 2.

1 broiler (2½ pounds)
Olive oil
1 tablespoon crushed red pepper flakes (or less, if a milder dish is wanted)

Salt
About ¼ cup dry white wine

Split chicken in half and crush flat (bones and all) with a meat mallet or a rolling pin. Brush both sides lavishly with olive oil. Sprinkle with red pepper flakes and salt. Preheat broiler and broil chicken not too close to the heat. Cook about 15 minutes on each side, basting with a little more oil. The chicken should be golden—take care not to burn. Transfer chicken to hot dish and keep hot. Place broiler pan with chicken juices over direct moderate heat and stir in wine. Bring to a boil and pour sauce over chicken. In Rome, this dish would be served with a tossed green salad.

Note: A very good variation of pollo alla diavola can be made by substituting an equal amount of crushed rosemary leaves, dried or fresh, for the red pepper flakes.

Chicken Livers with Sage I

(FEGATINI DI POLLO ALLA SALVIA)

Chicken livers and fresh sage are a great flavor combination, typical of Tuscany and Rome. Dried sage can be used in a pinch, but it is worthwhile to take the trouble to find fresh sage for this dish.

1 pound chicken livers	¼ cup butter
Salt and pepper	2 slices bacon, diced
12 chopped fresh sage leaves	¼ cup dry white wine
or 1 tablespoon dried sage	

Cut chicken livers into halves if they are large. Season with salt and pepper and coat with fresh or dried sage. Heat butter and bacon together in skillet. Sauté livers 5 to 6 minutes. Add white wine and simmer 2 minutes longer. Serve on spaghetti, rice or polenta.

Chicken Livers with Sage II
(SPIEDINO DI FEGATINI DI POLLO CON SALVIA)

In this version of the dish, the chicken livers are cooked on small skewers. Keep livers whole, season with salt and pepper and coat with chopped fresh or dried sage. Wrap livers in strips of Italian prosciutto or bacon. If Italian prosciutto is used, all fat must be trimmed off. String on small skewers. Broil over a campfire, a grill, a rotisserie, or in the oven.

If the livers are wrapped in bacon, there is no need for basting. But if lean Italian prosciutto covers the livers, the skewers should be basted with melted butter.

Milan Fried Chicken or Turkey Breasts
(PETTI DI POLLO O DI TACCHINO ALLA MILANESE)

This is perhaps *the* party dish from Milan, especially when made with turkey breasts.

Since the size of chicken breasts is more predictable than that of turkey breasts, the recipe below has been adjusted to them. If turkey breasts are used, they should be cut into the size of a *suprême*—that is, ½ a chicken breast; 1 whole breast makes 2 suprêmes. The recipe serves 4.

4 chicken breasts halved, skinned and boned	*2 eggs, well beaten*
Salt	*Very fine dry white bread crumbs*
Pepper	*¼ cup butter*
Flour	*3 tablespoons olive oil*

Trim chicken breasts and flatten them as thinly as possible with a rolling pin. The breasts should be as even in size as possible.

Season with salt and pepper. Dip in flour and shake off excess. Dip in beaten egg and bread crumbs. Shake dry. (This can be done before cooking time and the breasts stored in the refrigerator.) Heat butter and oil in large skillet. When fat is no longer bubbling but not brown, put in chicken breasts. Cook over heat that is a little hotter than moderate (but not too high) for about 4 to 7 minutes on each side (depending on size), or until golden. Dry on absorbent paper and serve very hot, garnished with parsley and lemon slices. Any of the nicer green vegetables, such as asparagus or tiny peas cooked with ham, would be a good accompaniment.

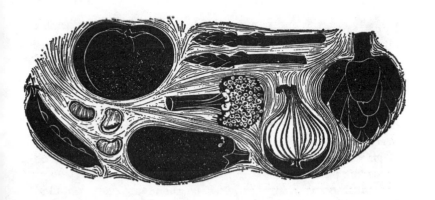

VEGETABLES

VEGETABLES FORM A VERY LARGE PART of the Italian diet, and
the Italians are very particular about their size, taste and
freshness. With the exception of lima beans, all the vegetables
we know in America can be found in Italy. Very often there are
several varieties of each kind, and almost always they are
young and small, so as to be tender as well as freshly picked.

In spite of the advent of refrigerators and frozen foods,
the Italians still insist on fresh vegetables, preferably bought
daily. The market stalls and greengrocers' displays are a lovely
sight to behold, one colorful tapestry that warms the cockles
of even a vegetable-hater's heart. A very special treat is the
primizie, the first new vegetables of a season, extra-tiny, extra-
tender.

Green vegetables, such as spinach, broccoli and green

beans, are often just boiled in a little water and served with oil and lemon. Stuffable vegetables such as eggplant, tomatoes and peppers are stuffed and fragrant with herbs; vegetables are also made into sformati, that is, vegetable puddings, held together by a sauce or eggs.

Often vegetables are served as a separate course, especially asparagus. Potatoes are seldom served if a pasta or rice preceded the meat course, and any meat course comes very often with just a salad, or with potatoes only, if there was no preceding pasta or rice.

Mushrooms, many varieties of them, are very popular, both fresh and dried. And a special accolade must go to the white truffles of Alba in Piedmont, more delicate than the black variety and the very best thing in the world for any dish.

GLOBE ARTICHOKES
(Carciofi)

Globe artichokes belong to the thistle family; the other kind, not very common in America, is the Jerusalem artichoke, a tuber which has no relation at all to the popular green, spiky globe. Artichokes are among the most popular of all Italian vegetables, cooked in a great many ways, and frequently with other ingredients. Here in America the large variety is the most common one, but there are others, small ones, which in Italy are to be found everywhere, and here only in markets in Italian neighborhoods. Unfortunately, the small, purple and deliciously tender Venetian artichoke is unknown in the United States.

Many Italian recipes for artichokes cannot be made with our variety. For instance, the most famous Roman artichoke dish is carciofi alla giudea, whole, deep-fried artichokes, which are pure delight. But for this you need especially tender, un-choky artichokes, which can be cooked whole, and we simply haven't got them.

Most Americans know of only one way of eating arti-chokes, that is, boiled, with a sauce to dip the leaves in. This is good, and it would also be worth doing the same with a tender, raw artichoke. The generally inhospitable look of an artichoke discourages people from preparing the vegetable for other kinds of cookery. Yet it is very simple, if two points are borne in mind. First, a whole lot of artichoke is waste, because it is tough and bitter. Second, artichokes discolor very easily, and as soon as they are cut up, they should be dropped into acidulated water, that is, water mixed with lemon juice or vinegar, which will keep them white. There are more involved ways of doing this, but they are quite unnecessary.

How to Prepare Artichokes

ACIDULATED WATER

Combine water and vinegar or lemon juice in a bowl. The proportion is 2 tablespoons of either to each quart of water.

HOW TO CUT UP ARTICHOKES

Prepare acidulated water. Have a sharp kitchen knife ready. Tear off and throw away the tough outer leaves, until leaves are greenish-white two thirds of the way up from the arti-choke's base. Lay artichoke on its side. Cut off green part of leaves with spikes in one stroke, leaving light part only. Dip artichoke in water. Cut off artichoke stem, leaving about ½ inch from the base. Peel base and remaining stem. Cut artichoke into four parts as you would cut an apple and work on one. Drop the other three parts into the acidulated water. Core each part, removing the fuzzy part or choke, as you would remove the core of an apple. Drop immediately back into acidulated water.

When the artichokes are small and very tender, they may be cooked cut into quarters. However, the vast majority of American artichokes are large and not tender. Therefore, the prepared quarters must be cut into thin slices, and the tougher the artichoke, the thinner the slices. Work quickly, so as not to discolor the slices unnecessarily by keeping them out in the air. Dry artichoke quarters or slices before cooking.

HOW TO PREPARE ARTICHOKE HEARTS OR BOTTOMS

Trim off stem flush with artichoke base. Tear off outer leaves, leaving only the inner fuzz. Cut off fuzz with a sharp knife. Drop into acidulated water. Dry before cooking.

WHICH FATS TO USE IN ARTICHOKE COOKERY

Artichokes have a robust flavor, and I think that cooking them with butter is not nearly as good as cooking them with olive oil. They seem to need the heartiness of olive oil. However, using only olive oil in braising artichokes would make for too rich a dish. Whenever artichokes are stewed in liquid, the liquid should be composed of even parts of olive oil and water or consommé.

Any cold sauce or dip to be used with plain boiled artichokes should be on the piquant side, such as a lemon mayonnaise or a Green Sauce.

Braised Artichokes

(STUFATINO DI CARCIOFI)

This is one of the simplest and most delicious ways of cooking artichokes; it is a method rather than a recipe, since the proportions of the ingredients depend on the size of the cooking utensil.

Depending on tenderness, cut artichokes into quarters or into thin slices. Put in heavy saucepan. Barely cover with an even mixture of olive oil and water. Season to taste with salt and pepper and any favorite herb, such as basil. Add minced parsley to taste. Simmer, covered, over lowest possible heat until artichokes are tender. Check occasionally for moisture; the finished dish should have just a little pan gravy. If it is too dry, add a little hot water; if too liquid, cook without cover to allow for evaporation. Serve with lemon wedges.

Note: A richer dish is made by using consommé instead of water.

VARIATIONS FOR BRAISED ARTICHOKES

1. Add ½ medium onion and/or a garlic glove. Remove garlic clove before serving.

2. For every medium artichoke, add about ½ cup fresh shelled peas or frozen peas to artichokes when they are half tender.

3. For every medium artichoke, add 2 tablespoons minced prosciutto or lean bacon to plain braised artichokes or to any of these variations.

4. Cook artichokes as in basic recipe. Drain and chill. Serve with a French dressing made with lemon juice and olive oil or with a piquant mayonnaise or cold sauce.

Peas with Prosciutto, Roman Fashion
(PISELLI CON PROSCIUTTO ALLA ROMANA)

3 tablespoons butter
3 tablespoons minced onion
⅓ cup diced Italian prosciutto,
    Canadian bacon or lean
    bacon

1½ to 2 pounds fresh peas,
    shelled or 1 10-ounce
    package frozen peas
2 to 4 tablespoons bouillon
Salt
Pepper

Combine butter, onion and prosciutto in heavy saucepan. Cook over medium heat, stirring constantly, for about 3 to 5 minutes, or until onion is tender. Add peas and bouillon. Season with salt and pepper to taste; the bouillon may be salty. Cook, covered, over low heat for about 10 minutes or until peas are tender. Cooking time depends on the quality of the peas. Stir occasionally; if necessary, add a little more bouillon, a tablespoon at a time.

Sweet-Sour Onions
(CIPOLLETTE ALL'AGRO)

Small white onions, preferably the pickling variety, should be used.

About 25 small white onions
3 tablespoons butter
1 tablespoon flour
1 cup bouillon or onion broth
1 tablespoon vinegar

1 to 2 teaspoons sugar
Salt
Pepper
1 tablespoon chopped parsley

Boil onions in salted water to cover until not quite tender. Drain, and reserve 1 cup of the broth. Heat 2 tablespoons of the butter and cook onions over low heat 3 to 4 minutes, or

until just golden. Remove onions and keep hot. Add remaining
1 tablespoon butter to skillet butter. Heat until golden, not
brown. Stir in flour and bouillon or onion broth. Cook over
low heat until thickened and smooth, stirring constantly. Add
vinegar, sugar, salt and pepper. Put onions back into sauce
and simmer, covered, for 5 minutes. Sprinkle with parsley
before serving.

Sicilian Baked Onions
(CIPOLLE AL FORNO)

Baked onions are absolutely delicious. Hot, they are eaten
with butter, salt and pepper, just like baked potatoes; cold,
with salt and pepper, a little olive oil and a squeeze of lemon
dribbled over them.

The onions must be unpeeled. Put medium-size or large
onions into a roasting pan and bake as you would potatoes,
for about 1 to 1½ hours. The skins then come off and the
onions are full of flavor.

Roman Stuffed Tomatoes
(POMODORI ALLA ROMANA)

On the food display tables of Roman restaurants, when the big
tomatoes which we call beefsteak tomatoes are in season, one
sees large pans of them stuffed with rice. The dish is an
unusually good one, and rather unknown outside Rome. It can
be eaten either hot or cold.

It is difficult to give very accurate amounts for the uncooked rice that is used to stuff the tomatoes, since the size of the latter varies so. Roughly speaking, about 2 tablespoons are needed if the tomatoes are very large. If any rice stuffing is left over, bake it alongside the tomatoes in the pan.

8 *medium-size to large tomatoes*	2 *cups hot chicken broth*
½ *cup olive oil*	Salt
⅓ *cup chopped parsley*	Pepper
2 *cloves garlic, minced*	⅛ *teaspoon cinnamon* (op-
1 *cup rice*	*tional*)

Cut a slice from the top of each tomato and scoop out center with a spoon without breaking the walls. Strain and save the juice. Place tomatoes in shallow baking dish. Sprinkle each tomato with a little olive oil—about 1 to 2 teaspoons.

Heat remaining oil in heavy saucepan. Cook parsley and garlic in it over medium heat 3 minutes. Add rice and cook 3 minutes longer, stirring constantly. Add hot chicken broth. Cover and cook 10 minutes, or until rice is three-quarters done. The cooking time varies with the kind of rice used. Remove from heat; season with salt and pepper and cinnamon. Fill tomatoes with rice mixture. Pour tomato juice over tomatoes to the depth of ½ to ¾ inch up the side of the tomatoes. Bake in moderate (350° F) oven 30 to 40 minutes, or until rice is tender and liquid absorbed. If during baking time the tomatoes show signs of drying out, add a little hot water. Baste occasionally.

Peppers, Roman Fashion

(PEPERONATA ALLA ROMANA)

A mixture of green, red and yellow sweet peppers is the most decorative. The cooking of Rome frequently uses lard, sometimes combined with olive oil, for a characteristic flavor.

4 *large peppers*
1 *tablespoon lard*
1 *tablespoon olive oil*
1 *small onion, diced*
3 *large tomatoes, peeled and chopped*

½ *teaspoon salt*
¼ *teaspoon pepper*
¼ *teaspoon basil or to taste* (*optional*)

Place peppers over high heat, directly on the burners, and roast until outer skin is black and blistered. Using your fingers, peel off outer skin under running cold water. Trim peppers free of membrane and seeds. Cut into strips. Dry thoroughly. In heavy saucepan, combine lard, oil and onion. Cook over low heat, stirring constantly, for about 3 minutes or until onion is soft. Add tomatoes and cook for 5 minutes. Add peppers, salt, pepper and basil. Simmer, covered, over low heat for 10 to 15 minutes, or until peppers are just tender. Stir frequently; if mixture is too thick, add a little hot water.

Green Beans with Cheese

(FAGIOLINI AL GROVIERA)

1 *pound green beans*
3 *tablespoons butter*
⅔ *cup grated Swiss cheese*

Salt
Pepper

Cook beans in boiling salted water until tender but still crisp. Drain. Heat butter in stove-to-table skillet but do not brown. Add beans and cook over medium heat, stirring constantly, for about 3 minutes. Sprinkle cheese, salt and pepper to taste, over beans and mix well. In a moment, there will be a golden crust at the bottom of the skillet, and the dish is ready for serving.

Fried Zucchini

(ZUCCHINE CROCCANTI)

Zucchini
Flour for dredging

Olive oil or shortening for frying
Parsley sprigs

Scrape zucchini lightly to remove wax coating on skins. Trim off top and blossom ends. Cut into halves lengthways. If zucchini are big, cut into quarters. Remove seeds. Cut zucchini into pieces the length of a thumb. Fill a bowl with water and add 2 to 3 tablespoons of salt for each quart of water. Soak zucchini in salted water for about 2 hours; this makes them firm. Rinse under running cold water and dry thoroughly with kitchen toweling. Dredge zucchini in flour and shake off excess flour. In large deep skillet, heat about 3 inches of olive oil or shortening. Olive oil will give a crisper result. Fry zucchini until golden brown and crisp. Fry a few at a time; they should not touch while frying. Drain on absorbent paper and keep hot. Last, fry parsley sprigs until crisp; this takes only about a minute. Drain and serve very hot, with lemon wedges.

Marinated Zucchini

(ZUCCHINE IN INSALATA)

This is a dish from Giannino, one of Milan's finest restaurants. It can also be made with yellow squash, or even eggplant, and will keep for at least three days in the refrigerator. Serve well chilled.

6 zucchini squash
Olive oil for frying
1 cup mild vinegar
½ cup olive oil
½ teaspoon garlic powder

6 chopped fresh basil leaves or
  1 tablespoon dried basil
Salt
Pepper
2 tablespoons chopped parsley

Trim zucchini, scrape lightly to remove waxy coating and cut into 1½-inch sticks—the size of a little finger. Fry slowly in olive oil until golden. Drain on absorbent paper. Combine vinegar, olive oil, garlic powder, basil, and salt and pepper to taste, and simmer 5 minutes. Arrange zucchini in layers in glass or china dish; do not use metal. Pour hot marinade over zucchini and sprinkle with parsley. Cover, and chill at least overnight. Drain before serving with roast or grilled meats or poultry.

Note: Do not overfry zucchini; they should have body and not be mushy.

Broccoli or Cauliflower, Roman Style

(BROCCOLI O CAVOLFIORI ALLA ROMANA)

1 medium-size bunch broccoli
  or 1 medium-size head
  cauliflower
¼ cup olive oil

2 garlic cloves
Salt
Pepper
1½ cups dry red or white wine

Trim broccoli or cauliflower and cut into small flowerets. Wash well and drain. Heat olive oil in large skillet and brown garlic. Remove garlic. Add vegetable, salt and pepper, and cook over medium heat 5 minutes. Add wine, cover skillet and simmer over low heat 10 to 15 minutes, or until vegetable is tender. Stir occasionally, taking care not to break flowerets.

Note: White wine is a better choice for cauliflower, since it will preserve the vegetable's white color.

String Beans, Wax Beans, Fava Beans, Lima Beans or Peas, with Ham

(LEGUMI CON PROSCIUTTO)

This is a method for cooking vegetables, rather than one single recipe, and it makes them more interesting. Prosciutto is used in Italy, of course, because it is more savory, but if none is available, use Canadian bacon or any cooked ham.

Cook vegetable in just enough water to prevent scorching until three-quarters done. Drain. For each pound of vegetable, heat together 2 tablespoons butter and 1 tablespoon oil. Sauté 2 teaspoons minced onion and ¼ teaspoon minced garlic. Stir in ½ cup chopped ham and cook 3 to 4 minutes. Add vegetable and season with salt and pepper. If necessary, add a little bouillon to prevent scorching while cooking. Cover and cook until tender, stirring occasionally. Before serving, sprinkle with 1 tablespoon finely chopped parsley.

Florentine Mushrooms

(FUNGHI TRIFOLATI)

1 pound mushrooms	1 tablespoon butter
3 tablespoons olive oil	4 anchovy fillets, chopped (optional)
1 clove garlic	
Salt	2 tablespoons chopped parsley
Pepper	Juice of ½ lemon

Slice mushrooms thinly. Heat olive oil in large skillet and brown garlic. Remove garlic. Add mushrooms, salt and pepper, and cook over high heat until all the mushroom liquid has evaporated. Add butter, anchovy fillets and parsley, and cook

over medium heat 5 minutes longer. Remove from fire, add
lemon juice and serve very hot.

Onions and Mushrooms
(CONTORNO DI CIPOLLE E FUNGHI)

A dish from the Abruzzi.

1 pound onions, thinly sliced
Boiling water
3 tablespoons olive oil
1 garlic clove, minced
¼ cup minced parsley

1 pound mushrooms, thickly
  sliced
1 tablespoon vinegar or more to
  taste

Cook onions in boiling water to cover until almost tender.
Drain. Heat olive oil. Cook, stirring constantly, garlic and
parsley in it for 2 minutes. Add mushrooms. Cook, over low
heat, stirring constantly, until mushrooms are half tender, and
their liquid has almost entirely evaporated. Add onions.
Simmer, covered, until vegetables are tender. Stir in vinegar.
Serve with roasted meats.

Potato Stew
(PATATE IN UMIDO)

2 pounds potatoes
¼ cup minced salt pork
2 tablespoons butter
1 medium onion, thinly sliced

1 clove garlic
1 1-pound can Italian tomatoes
Salt
Pepper

Peel potatoes and cut into ½-inch cubes. Heat together salt
pork and butter. Add onion and garlic. Cook until onion is

soft. Add tomatoes, potatoes and salt and pepper to taste. Cook over low heat, stirring frequently, until potatoes are tender. If necessary, to prevent sticking, add a little hot water. Remove garlic clove before serving. Serve with roast or broiled meats.

Note: Two to four dried mushrooms, soaked in water to cover and cut into pieces, may be added with their liquid to the potatoes at the same time as the tomatoes.

Truffled (Braised) Potatoes
(PATATE TRIFOLATE)

There are no truffles in this recipe; the term refers to the small pieces into which the potatoes are cut.

1½ to 2 pounds potatoes	*¼ cup minced parsley*
¼ cup olive oil	*⅔ cup bouillon*
1 small garlic clove, minced	*Salt*
	Pepper

Peel potatoes and cut into ⅛- to ¼-inch dice. Wash and dry well. Heat oil in heavy saucepan or casserole. Add potatoes. Cook over medium heat, stirring constantly, for about 5 minutes or until potatoes are half-cooked. Add garlic, parsley and bouillon. Season with salt and pepper to taste; go easy on the salt since the bouillon may be salty. Cook, covered, over low heat until potatoes are tender. Stir frequently. Serve with plain broiled or roasted meats.

Note: Different varieties of potatoes absorb liquids differently, and more bouillon may be needed. Add a little at a time. When finished, the potatoes should be dry, yet moist. If the dish is too liquid, finish cooking without cover, to allow for evaporation.

Tuscan Beans

(FAGIOLI ALL'UCCELLETTO)

This dish should be well-flavored with sage.

1½ cups dried white beans
2 tablespoons butter
3 tablespoons olive oil
2 tablespoons fresh sage,
    chopped, or ¾ teaspoon
    ground sage

Salt
Pepper
¼ to ⅓ cup tomato sauce

Soak beans overnight. Cook in boiling water to cover until beans are tender. This must be done over very low heat so that the beans will not burst open. Drain beans. Heat together butter and olive oil. Add beans, sage and salt and pepper to taste. Cook over medium heat, stirring constantly with a fork (so as not to break the beans) for 3 minutes. Add tomato sauce and cook for 2 minutes longer or until beans and sauce are very hot. Serve with boiled beef.

Lentil Purée

(PUREA DI LENTICCHIE)

The characteristic contorno, or side dish, for cotechino, or braised meats and poultry.

1½ cups dried lentils
About 5 cups liquid from the
    cotechino, or bouillon
1 small onion, sliced

¼ cup butter, melted
Salt
Pepper
⅛ teaspoon nutmeg

Combine lentils, cotechino liquid and onion. Simmer, covered, until lentils are extremely soft. Force through a strainer or purée in blender. Return to saucepan. Cook, stirring constantly, until surplus liquid has evaporated and lentils are a thick purée. Stir in butter, salt and pepper to taste and nutmeg. Serve very hot.

Note: The lentils may also be cooked in water. Since this would give them a flat taste—and lentils need robustness—add 6 slices of minced bacon or a hambone to the cooking liquid.

SAUCES

NOWHERE IS THE DIFFERENCE between French and Italian cooking more pronounced than in the sauces. Italian sauces are
simple and usually piquant, to add zest to the food rather than
to mask it. There are none of the French fumets, meat glazes
and sauces mères, no thickening with beurre manié and with
cream. And when there is, the sauce is of French origin.

With the exception of white sauce (called by its French
name of Béchamel in Italy), which is frequently used, Italian
sauces are generally amusing, fragrant and easy to make. It is
most unfortunate that so many non-Italians, who've never been
to the country, think of tomato sauce as the only Italian sauce.
Of course it is frequently used, but never drenching a food as
it does outside of Italy. And the best tomato sauces are the
ones that are quickly cooked, so that the tomatoes retain their
fresh flavor. A little fresh cream or butter, stirred into a finished

tomato sauce, does wonders for it, removing the somewhat acid taste of all tomato sauces. Among tomato sauces, the famous Ragú alla Bolognese towers over all others; it is a truly great sauce.

Sugo generally means a meat sauce, or rather, an essence of meat. There is no literal translation for the word, which means juice, gravy having quite a different consistency, since it is thickened with flour. The closest would be the French *jus*.

The farther south you go in Italy, the richer the tomato sauces. But the meat tomato sauce so beloved in the United States is far more American than Italian.

Neapolitan Pizzaiola Sauce

The tomatoes are cooked just long enough to soften, but they must not be overcooked, or the sauce will lose its very fresh taste. Pizzaiola sauce is usually served on steaks, but it is excellent on the lighter pasta varieties, such as spaghetti, linguine or thin noodles.

¼ cup olive oil
1½ to 2 pounds fresh tomatoes, peeled, seeded and chopped
2 cloves garlic, minced
Salt

Pepper
1 teaspoon dried oregano or 1 tablespoon chopped fresh basil or 2 tablespoons chopped parsley

Heat olive oil in heavy saucepan. Add tomatoes, garlic, salt and pepper to taste, and herb. Cook over high heat about 10 to 15 minutes, or until tomatoes are just soft.

Meat Sauce from Bologna
(RAGÚ ALLA BOLOGNESE)

This sauce no more resembles an ordinary tomato sauce than a goose resembles a swan. It is a classic of Italian cookery.

¼ pound prosciutto or bacon, minced
1 tablespoon butter
1 medium onion, minced
1 carrot, minced
¼ stalk celery, minced
½ pound lean beef, ground twice
¼ pound chicken livers, minced

1 cup dry white wine
1 cup beef bouillon
2 tablespoons tomato paste
Salt
Pepper
⅛ teaspoon ground nutmeg
2 teaspoons grated lemon rind
2 cloves
1 cup heavy cream

On chopping board, combine prosciutto, butter, onion, carrot and celery. With a sharp knife, mince together to make almost a paste. In a heavy saucepan, cook the mixture over low heat until slightly browned. Add beef and brown evenly. Add chicken livers and cook for 2 minutes. Combine wine, bouillon and tomato paste and blend well. Add to meat mixture. Season with salt and pepper to taste. Stir in nutmeg, grated lemon rind and add cloves. Simmer covered over lowest possible heat for 45 minutes, stirring occasionally. At serving time, heat cream but do not let it boil. Stir hot cream into sauce.

Stracotto Meat Sauce for All Pasta, Rice and Polenta
(LO STRACOTTO)

Stracotto means overcooked in Italian, and overcooking is the secret behind this sauce, one of the very best in Italian cookery. What it really is can be described as a very flavorful essence of meat which has been cooked with mushrooms and Marsala. The sauce must be free of fat, and the only way of achieving this is to get the very leanest, top-quality steak. As for mushrooms, the dried, imported variety is preferable to the fresh kind we buy in the stores, since these imported mushrooms have an infinitely more fragrant taste. Dry red wine may be used instead of Marsala, but Marsala gives by far the best flavor to the sauce.

1½ to 2 ounces dried mush-
rooms
1 pound top quality beef
½ cup butter
1 medium onion, minced
1 medium carrot, minced
1 stalk celery, minced
½ cup minced parsley
⅔ cup dry Marsala
1 cup consommé
Salt
Pepper
1 teaspoon grated lemon rind

Crumble mushrooms and soak in water to cover. Cut meat into smallest possible dice—it must not be ground like hamburger. In heavy saucepan, heat butter. Add onion, carrot, celery and parsley. Cook over medium heat, stirring constantly, for about 3 minutes. Add mushrooms and their liquid, wine and consommé. Season with salt and pepper to taste and add lemon rind. Cover tightly. Simmer over lowest possible heat, and preferably on an asbestos plate, until the meat has almost dissolved. Stir frequently. This should take about 3 hours; this length of time is necessary for the flavors to blend. The sauce should be thick; if too thin, cook uncovered to allow for evaporation. Enough for 1 to 1½ pounds of pasta.

Anchovy Sauce
(SALSA DI ALICI)

For pasta, fish, sea food and boiled meats.

¼ cup olive oil
¼ cup butter
2 to 4 garlic cloves, minced

1 to 2 cans (2 ounces each) anchovies, drained or 1 tablespoon anchovy paste or anchovies to taste
⅓ cup minced parsley

Heat together olive oil, butter and garlic. Cook over low heat, stirring constantly, until garlic is extremely soft. Add anchovies. Cook, stirring constantly, until the anchovies are a soft paste. Stir in parsley. Makes about ¾ cup sauce.

Simple Caper Sauce
(SALSA SEMPLICE CON I CAPPERI)

For fish and sea food, plain meats and vegetables.

½ cup olive oil
½ cup drained capers

Juice of 1 lemon
Pepper

Combine olive oil, capers and lemon juice and mix well. Season to taste with pepper. Makes about ¾ cup sauce.

Evelina's Pasta Condiments
(I CONDIMENTI DI EVELINA)

Evelina, a splendid cook in Rome, keeps these two condiments on the table when she serves pasta, so that people can add a little of either one, in order to pep up the dish.

HOT PEPPER CONDIMENT
(CONDIMENTO ALLA DIAVOLO)

2 small hot red peppers   *Olive oil to cover*

Mince peppers, seeds and all, as finely as possible. Put them into a small earthenware or glass jar, such as a mustard jar. Cover with about 2 inches of olive oil. Use by the dropful on any pasta or rice sauce.

Note: Hot red peppers can be bought in Italian, Spanish and gourmet stores.

ROMAN ANCHOVY BUTTER
(BURRO D'ALICI ALLA ROMANA)

½ cup butter, creamed   *Anchovy paste to taste*

Cream butter with 1 teaspoon of anchovy paste until smooth. Add anchovy paste to taste. The mixture must be smoothly blended.

Note: This Anchovy Butter is excellent for boiled fish and sea food, and for hard-cooked eggs.

Zucchini Sauce

(SALSA DI ZUCCHINE)

¼ cup olive oil
¼ cup butter
½ cup minced onions
1 garlic clove
½ cup minced pepper

1½ to 2 pounds zucchini
    squash, sliced
3 cups tomatoes, peeled, seeded
    and chopped
1 teaspoon salt
½ teaspoon pepper

Heat olive oil and butter over medium heat. Cook onions in it for 2 minutes. Add all other ingredients. Cook, covered, over low heat about 30 minutes, stirring frequently. Zucchini should be tender, but still preserve their shape. Good for ziti, mezzani and other short-cut pasta. Enough for 1 pound of pasta.

VARIATION

½ pound sliced mushrooms, sautéed in 2 tablespoons olive oil, may be added to sauce for the last 10 minutes of cooking time.

Mushroom Spaghetti Sauce

(SALSA DI FUNGHI PER SPAGHETTI)

4 medium-size onions, thinly
    sliced
6 tablespoons butter
2 pounds fresh mushrooms,
    sliced

Salt
Pepper
¼ teaspoon nutmeg
1 cup heavy cream

In a heavy skillet, melt 3 tablespoons of the butter. Sauté onions in it over medium heat 5 to 7 minutes, or until golden brown, stirring frequently. Cover and cook onions over very low heat 30 minutes, or until very soft. Stir occasionally. Melt remaining butter in another skillet and sauté the mushrooms until tender. Season with salt, pepper and nutmeg; add to onions. Keep sauce hot while spaghetti is cooking according to package directions. Five minutes before serving, add cream to sauce and heat through. Do not boil or the sauce will curdle. Mix cooked spaghetti and sauce thoroughly and serve immediately with grated Parmesan cheese.

Note: This amount of sauce is sufficient for 1 pound of spaghetti or linguine.

Chicken-Liver Sauce for Spaghetti, Risotto, Polenta
(SALSA DI FEGATINI DI POLLO)

¼ pound lean bacon, minced
1 small onion, minced
¼ cup minced parsley
½ minced garlic clove (optional)
1 pound chicken livers, halved or cut into quarters

½ pound mushrooms, thinly sliced
¼ cup dry white wine or Marsala
½ teaspoon ground sage or dried sage leaves to taste
Salt
Pepper

On a chopping board, mince together minced bacon, onion, parsley and garlic clove to make a paste. Put into deep skillet. Heat and cook, stirring constantly, for 5 minutes. Add the chicken livers and mushrooms. Cook over medium heat, stirring constantly, for 3 minutes or until the livers are browned. Add wine, sage, salt and pepper. Cook, stirring constantly, for 3 minutes longer. Enough for 1 to 1½ pounds of pasta.

Hot Piquant Sauce

(SALSA PICCANTE CALDA)

For broiled meats, cold meats and vegetables such as cauliflower, broccoli and asparagus.

⅓ cup minced prosciutto or Canadian bacon
2 tablespoons minced onion
2 tablespoons minced parsley
2 tablespoons minced celery
½ minced garlic clove
1 clove
1 bay leaf
½ teaspoon salt
¼ teaspoon pepper
1½ cups mild vinegar
1 cup bouillon
1 tablespoon flour
2 teaspoons water
1 teaspoon prepared mustard
2 tablespoons drained capers
2 tablespoons butter, cut into small pieces

In heavy saucepan, combine prosciutto, onion, parsley, celery, garlic clove, clove, bay leaf, salt, pepper and vinegar. Simmer, covered, over low heat for about 15 minutes, or until the vinegar is reduced to about ½ cup. In top of double boiler, heat bouillon. Mix flour and water to a smooth paste. Stir flour paste into hot bouillon, beating until smooth and thickened. Cook over boiling water for 5 minutes. Strain vinegar mixture and add to bouillon. Stir in mustard and add capers. Simmer, covered, for 10 minutes. Before serving time, add butter. Stir until the butter is dissolved and the sauce hot. Makes about 1⅔ cups sauce.

Note: The sauce may be refrigerated and heated again over boiling water. The sauce itself should not boil.

Rita's Mushroom Sauce

(SALSA DI FUNGHI ALLA RITA)

1 tablespoon minced onion	*1 tablespoon flour*
2 tablespoons minced parsley	*1 tomato, peeled, seeded and*
½ cup minced prosciutto or	*chopped*
lean bacon	*1 cup dry white wine*
2 tablespoons olive oil	*½ cup bouillon*
2 tablespoons butter	*Salt*
½ pound mushrooms, sliced	*Pepper*

Combine onion, parsley and prosciutto on chopping board. Chop together so that the ingredients are well blended and form a paste. Heat olive oil and butter. Over low heat, stirring constantly, cook onion mixture for 5 minutes. Add mushrooms and cook, over medium heat, stirring constantly, for 3 minutes. Stir in flour. Add tomato, wine, bouillon and salt and pepper to taste. Simmer, covered, for 10 minutes. Serve with plain roasted or broiled meats and poultry.

Thin Egg and Lemon Sauce for Vegetables

(SALSA PER VERDURE IN LESSO)

One of the very simplest and very best sauces for plain boiled vegetables.

In a bowl, beat 1 egg yolk with the juice of ½ lemon. Season with salt and pepper to taste. Pour over drained hot vegetables. Enough for about 2 to 2½ cups boiled vegetables.

Uncooked Sweet Pepper Sauce
(SALSETTA AI PEPERONI)

The big red or yellow sweet peppers, which are very juicy and fleshy, may be used or combined with green peppers.

2 large peppers
1 medium onion
½ to ⅔ cup olive oil

1 tablespoon mild vinegar or vinegar or lemon juice to taste
Salt
Pepper

Peel peppers as described on page 123. Trim off inner membranes. Chop together peppers and onion until the size of peas. Add olive oil, vinegar, and salt and pepper to taste. Mix well. Serve with broiled meats, chicken, fish and sea food. Makes about 1½ cups sauce.

Uncooked Piquant Green Sauce
(SALSA VERDE PICCANTE)

A classic sauce of Italian cookery, found in all regions, with slight variations. This is the recipe of the great nineteenth-century cook Artusi, the dean of classic Italian cookery. An electric blender is ideal for this sauce, since it eliminates much tiresome chopping and mincing. The sauce is excellent for hot and cold boiled and broiled meats, sea food, hard-cooked eggs (as an antipasto) and cooked vegetables such as artichokes, cardoons, cauliflower and broccoli.

2 tablespoons drained capers
1 tablespoon minced onion
1 minced garlic clove
1 anchovy, chopped
2 cups parsley heads without
    stems, tightly packed

1 teaspoon dried basil or fresh
    basil to taste
¾ cup olive oil
Juice of 2 lemons
1 teaspoon salt
¼ teaspoon pepper

Combine all ingredients in a blender. Blend to a purée. Or mince together to a pulp the capers, onion, garlic clove and anchovy. Mince together until very fine the parsley and basil. Combine with the caper mixture. Slowly beat in oil, lemon juice, salt and pepper. Blend thoroughly. Makes about 1⅛ cups sauce.

VARIATIONS

Add a chopped hard-cooked egg, or ⅓ cup chopped walnuts or pignoli nuts to sauce.

Basil Sauce

(PESTO ALLA GENOVESE)

A Genoese specialty for pasta. The basil *must* be fresh.

3 to 5 cloves garlic, minced
¼ to ⅔ cup fresh basil leaves,
    minced

¼ cup grated Romano and
    Parmesan cheese, mixed
¼ cup chopped pine nuts
6 tablespoons olive oil

In a mortar, pound all ingredients except the olive oil into a smooth paste. Or use an electric blender. Gradually add olive oil to this paste, a few drops at a time, stirring constantly until the sauce is smooth and thick. Makes about ⅔ cup sauce.

Note: Pesto can be stored in the refrigerator in a jar, covered with olive oil. When adding it to cooked pasta, add a lump of butter at the same time.

Bagna Cauda

A sauce or dip from Piedmont, whose name means, literally, a hot bath. Good for raw or plain boiled vegetables, boiled fish and meats, which are dipped in it. A small sliced truffle improves the sauce greatly.

½ cup butter
¼ cup olive oil
6 cloves garlic, sliced paper-
 thin

2 2-ounce cans anchovy fillets
 (without capers), minced

Over lowest possible heat (you may have to use an asbestos mat), cook together butter, olive oil, and garlic for 15 minutes. Do not let boil. Stir in anchovy fillets and simmer until they dissolve. Keep the sauce hot over a candle or alcohol plate warmer. *The sauce must never boil or brown.* Makes about ¾ cup sauce.

DESSERTS AND CAKES

THE STANDARD ENDING to an Italian meal is not a dessert, but cheese and fruit, or fruit alone. Usually the Italians eat fresh fruit, but a fruit salad, or nowadays even canned fruit, might come to the table. Oranges, apples, pears, figs, grapes—whatever fruits are in season—are served; in a restaurant, the diner chooses his own from a basket piled high with perfect fruit. Thus fruit is more than an incidental, as it is so often in the United States; it is an integral part of the meal.

Formerly—and formerly means roughly until the end of World War I, when the old Italian living order changed from inside out—desserts were a great treat, and not lightly served. A custard, a tart, a creamy dessert appeared on special, much-looked-forward-to occasions. As time has gone on, and especially since women's magazines have become both very numerous and popular, desserts appear far more frequently, especially the packaged puddings that delight children. In my childhood, vanilla or chocolate puddings were an almost unknown treat since these puddings had to be imported from Germany. As for gelatin desserts, they were something extra-special; when I first came to the United States, fully grown and earning my own living, for months on end I could not eat my fill of Jell-O. But the current young in Italy, or rather of the Italian middle classes, know these delights, though they are not daily pleasures, fruit being still king of desserts.

Home baking has seen a similar evolution. Formerly, there was very little of it, and it consisted of cakes and cookies with an almost archaic and patriarchal flavor that tied in with the special holidays to which they belonged. Nowadays, Italian women, forced into their own kitchens by the lack of the formerly plentiful servants, have become very much interested in baking, thanks again to the women's magazines. But this too is a middle-class habit rather than a universal one, and it is found in Northern Italy rather than in the South.

All Italians love sweet things, but they don't have to be made at home. Italian pastry cooks and confectioners have been famous since the Venetian traders first brought sugar to Europe from the East in the Middle Ages. Earlier, all the sweetening had been done with honey, and honey continued to be the sweetening of the masses long after. Italian pasticcieri are still famous, and a good Italian pasticcieria is one of the things that make living worthwhile. They can be found in all the cities, with dozens and dozens of superlatively delicious *paste*, somewhat similar to French pastries but much smaller in size and infinitely more varied. Nowadays they even make *paste mignon*, miniature morsels of infinite delight. Pasticcierie resemble cafés, with tables inside or on the sidewalks. Italian ladies go there to take their afternoon tea, with cakes; men stop for coffee, with cakes; children are taken to eat ices, with cakes. They are indeed one of the pleasures of Italian living.

Here you can find also beautiful big cakes, many of which resemble ornate architectural structures with their decorations of candied fruits, glazes and spun sugar. To this day, it is far more elegant for an Italian hostess to order a St. Honoré or some extra fancy *paste* from a famous shop than to make her own for her dinner parties.

The same goes for ice cream. Italian ice cream is not the plain, rich kind like ours, which all Italians justly consider far superior to their own cream ices, and on which they gorge themselves when they come to America. Italian cassate, spumoni, etc., are generally composed of a mixture of flavors, including a tart fruit flavor. I think the most excellent of all Italian ices are the ones made with fresh fruit, or with coffee. These are very easily made at home, as in the recipes that follow, but the fruit must be good and flavorful.

Italian desserts, both those eaten with a spoon and cakes, can be very different indeed in the various regions of the country. Those specialties are very much worth investigating on the spot; many of them reach back many centuries.

Also, one should not forget the Italian preserved fruit, i frutti glacé, including the marrons glacées, which are superlative.

As for preserving and making jams, this is not an ingrained habit as it is in the Germanic and Northern European countries, and in ours. Sugar is still far more expensive than in the United States, and since Italians are not big jam eaters, most prefer to buy what they need.

Rum Cake

(DOLCE AL RUM)

This is the kind of cake Italians order from a pasticceria for their dinner parties.

CAKE

3 *eggs*
1 *cup sugar*
3 *tablespoons cold water*

2 *teaspoons vanilla*
1 *cup sifted all-purpose flour*
2 *teaspoons baking powder*

Beat eggs until light. Gradually beat in the sugar and continue beating until mixture is thick and pale in color. Use an electric beater for this, if possible, and beat on high speed 6 minutes. Stir in the water and vanilla. Sift flour with baking powder three times and fold into batter. Pour into buttered and floured 9-inch spring-form pan and bake in preheated moderate oven (350° F.) 30 minutes, or until cake tests clean. Cool in pan while making the topping.

TOPPING

1 *tablespoon (1 envelope)*
   gelatin
¼ *cup cold water*
2 *cups hot milk*
¾ *cup sugar*

4 *egg yolks, lightly beaten*
⅓ *cup dark rum*
1 *large orange*
1 *cup heavy cream*

Soften gelatin in cold water for a few minutes. Stir in hot milk and sugar and cook over low heat until mixture is hot. It must not boil. Gradually pour over egg yolks, stirring constantly. Add rum. Set pan in bowl of cracked ice and stir constantly until cool and beginning to set. Peel orange free of all yellow and white peel and skin and separate into segments. Fold orange segments and cream into custard. Pour over cooled cake in the pan and chill until serving time. To serve, remove cake from pan and garnish with orange slices, glacé cherries and rosettes of whipped cream.

Chocolate Dessert
(DOLCE TORINO)

24 ladyfingers
1 cup brandy or rum
½ teaspoon vanilla
½ pound semisweet chocolate
3 to 4 tablespoons light cream
1 cup sweet butter (it must be sweet butter)

⅓ cup sugar
2 egg yolks, slightly beaten
Blanched almond halves
Glacé cherries
Whipped cream

Split ladyfingers and place on platter. Pour brandy or rum over them and let soak for at least 2 hours. They should be well drenched with liquor but still retain their shape. Combine vanilla, chocolate and cream in top of double boiler. Melt over hot water. Cream together butter and sugar until light and thoroughly blended. The sugar should no longer be grainy. Gradually add egg yolks, mixing well. Add chocolate mixture to butter mixture, a little at a time, blending thoroughly, until the whole is soft and creamy. Do not undermix.

On a glass or, preferably, a silver serving dish, arrange a layer of ladyfingers in the form of a square. Cover with a thin layer of chocolate cream. Repeat process, finishing with a layer of chocolate. Reserve a little chocolate cream to coat sides. Smooth chocolate surface with a wet knife. Decorate top with blanched almond halves and glacé cherries cut into halves. Let ripen in a cool place for at least 12 hours. At serving time, pipe whipped cream in decorative swags around the border of the cake.

Note: The reason for keeping the dolce torino in a cool place rather than in the refrigerator is that too cold a temperature congeals the butter. However, if it must be kept in the refrigerator, let it stand at room temperature at least 30 minutes before serving.

Mont Blanc of Chestnuts

One of the world's greatest desserts. To be at its peak, it ought to be made only a short time before serving.

Score chestnuts across rounded side with a sharp knife. Place in boiling water and simmer for 15 minutes. Drain, but keep warm. Slip off both skins. Return to pan, cover with boiling water, and simmer for about 45 minutes, or until perfectly tender. Drain and mash with a little salt and with sugar to taste. Over a large serving dish (perferably silver) force chestnuts through a coarse sieve, a potato ricer or a food mill with fairly large holes, into the shape of a mound. The chestnuts must be very light and fluffy.

Whip some heavy cream and flavor with a little sugar and vanilla. Smooth cream over chestnut mound. Do not press down, or the Mont Blanc will loose its fluffiness. Chill for a short time and serve.

Note: Some Mont Blanc recipes suggest simmering the chestnuts in a light sugar syrup. I have found this to impair the essential fluffiness of the dessert.

Zabaglione

This is another of the world's great desserts. The combination of eggs, sugar and spirits occurs in countries other than Italy, but nowhere else is the formula so happy. In a pinch, sherry can be used instead of Marsala, but the genuine zabaglione must have Marsala. The following recipe is for 3.

4 egg yolks   *¾ cup Marsala*
¾ cup sugar

Combine ingredients in the top of a double boiler. Cook over simmering, but not boiling, water, beating constantly with a wire whisk or an egg beater, for about 10 minutes, or until very thick. Serve immediately in glasses or small coffee cups.

COLD ZABAGLIONE

Proceed as above. Set pan in a basin filled with cracked ice. Beat zabaglione until thoroughly cold. Pour into glasses or cups and keep refrigerated.

Note: Unless the zabaglione is beaten until thoroughly cold, it will not remain frothy but will collapse and separate.

Fruit Salad
(MACEDONIA DI FRUTTA)

A macedonia is a mixture; it may be of vegetables or fruits. There are no set proportions for this extremely popular Italian dessert. Whatever fruits are available, such as peaches, pears, apricots, plums, apples and oranges, are peeled and cut into bite-size pieces. Strawberries and raspberries, when in season, are added to the mixture. So are a few coarsely chopped walnuts, blanched almonds cut into strips and pistachio nuts. The fruits are placed in a glass dish and sprinkled with sugar. They may be dressed with a glass of sweet wine, or a little Kirsch or Maraschino or other liqueur. For festive occasions, champagne is used instead of other spirits. A macedonia is served well chilled, as is, or with a garnish of whipped cream.

Sliced Oranges and Apples with Marsala or Sherry
(MELE E ARANCE AL MARSALA)

Slice the oranges into thin, round slices, taking care to remove all white skin and pips. Core but do not peel the apples and slice into rounds. Sprinkle with powdered sugar and add a generous amount of Marsala or sherry. Chill for several hours before serving, so that the wine has a chance to penetrate the fruit.

Baked Peaches
(PESCHE RIPIENE)

A classic Italian dessert. The peaches must be large and ripe but still firm. Freestone peaches are best.

4 large peaches	*¼ cup mixed glacé fruit,*
½ cup almond macaroon	*shredded fine*
crumbs or ground almonds	*8 blanched almonds*
	Marsala or white wine

Halve peaches. Remove pits and enlarge hollow slightly with a spoon. Mash this extra pulp and combine it with macaroon crumbs or ground almonds and glacé fruit. Fill peach hollows with this mixture. Butter a deep baking dish. Place peaches in dish. Top each peach half with 1 almond. Sprinkle with Marsala or white wine. Bake in moderate (350° F.) oven for 15 to 20 minutes, or until just tender. Check for dryness—if necessary, add a little Marsala diluted with water, or some wine. Serve hot or cold.

Strawberries with Marsala

(FRAGOLE AL MARSALA)

The best Italian strawberries are the tiny wild ones whose perfume fills a room and which is even more enchanting than their taste. Since water destroys a good part of a strawberry's aroma, the Italians usually wash theirs in wine.

Strawberries are sprinkled with sugar and Marsala (or white or red wine) and kept in a cool place several hours before serving, since chilling (at least excessive chilling) kills their flavor. Another good way of serving them is to sprinkle them with sugar and either lemon or orange juice.

Chestnuts with Marsala and Wine

(CASTAGNE AL MARSALA)

1 pound chestnuts   *1 cup red wine*
½ cup sugar   *1 cup Marsala*

Score chestnuts across rounded side with a sharp knife. Place in boiling water and simmer for 15 minutes. Drain, but keep warm. Slip off both skins. The skins should come off quite easily, provided the chestnuts are warm. Work carefully, since chestnuts break very easily.

Combine sugar, red wine and Marsala, and cook, covered, over low heat for 5 minutes. Carefully place chestnuts in pan and simmer until tender. Shake pan occasionally so that chestnuts won't stick. Lift chestnuts with a slotted spoon and place in glass or silver serving dish. Reduce syrup and pour over chestnuts. Serve with plain heavy cream and thin, crisp cookies.

Flamed Chestnuts

(CASTAGNE ALLA FIAMMA)

Delicious with wine, the way they are served in country inns in the Abruzzi.

Place roasted and peeled chestnuts on a platter and sprinkle sugar over them. Pour rum or Marsala over chestnuts and blaze.

Water Ices

(GRANITE)

Most refreshing on a hot day, granite are made with water and flavorings only. They are admirably suited to being made in the refrigerator, since they do not have to be stirred as often as cream ices to avoid the formation of ice crystals. These crystals are part of a granita, which is frozen the same way as ice cubes. The freezing time, though, will be longer, because of the sugar in the granita.

Strawberry or Raspberry Ice

(GRANITA DI FRAGOLE O DI LAMPONI)

2 quarts fresh strawberries or raspberries	1 cup water
1 cup sugar	Juice of 1 small lemon

Strain berries through a fine sieve or purée in a blender. Boil sugar and water together for 5 minutes. Cool. Combine with berry purée and stir in lemon juice. Freeze, stirring occasionally.

Lemon Ice
(GRANITA DI LIMONE)

1¼ cups lemon juice (or more,   *3 cups water*
*   if a tarter ice is wanted)*   *⅔ cup sugar*
Grated rind of 1 lemon

Combine lemon juice and rind. Boil water and sugar together for 5 minutes. Cool, then stir in lemon juice. Freeze, stirring occasionally.

Coffee Ice with Cream
(GRANITA DI CAFFÈ CON PANNA)

1½ cups ground Italian-style   *5 cups boiling water*
*   coffee*
⅓ cup sugar

Combine coffee, sugar and water in top of double boiler. Steep, over simmering water, 30 minutes. Cool. Strain through a strainer lined with a triple thickness of cheesecloth. Freeze in ice tray at regular freezing temperature. Stir occasionally. Serve in tall glasses, topped with sweetened whipped cream.

Cold Zabaglione Cream
(SEMIFREDDO DI ZABAGLIONE)

A rich and elegant party dessert.

1 *envelope unflavored gelatin*
3 *tablespoons water*
5 *egg yolks*
5 *tablespoons sugar*
10 *tablespoons dry Marsala or dry white wine*

1 *egg white, beaten*
1½ *cups heavy cream, whipped*
Whipped cream, candied violets for decorating

Sprinkle gelatin over water. Set in a pan with hot water. Heat until gelatin is liquid. Keep it liquid. In top of 1½-quart double boiler, combine eggs yolks and sugar. Beat (preferably with electric beater at high speed) until mixture is thick and white. Beat in Marsala or wine. Place over, but *not in*, gently boiling water. Beat constantly until mixture is thick and has risen to edges of container. Beat in gelatin. Fill a container with ice cubes and water. Set top of double boiler in it. Mixture will collapse on contact with the cold. Continue beating until zabaglione is thoroughly cold. Beat egg white until stiff. Gently fold into zabaglione. Fold in whipped cream. Pour into serving dish or individual dessert dishes. Chill for 2 hours before serving. Decorate with rosettes or swirls of whipped cream and candied violets. Serve with crisp plain cookies. Makes 6 to 8 servings.

Homemade Ice Cream with Almonds
(SPUMONE GELATO ALLE MANDORLE)

The texture of this dish should be spongy but firm.

3 cups heavy cream
¾ cup sugar, sifted
1¼ cups blanched almonds,
    shredded and toasted

4 ounces (4 squares) semisweet
    chocolate, chopped fine
1 tablespoon brandy (optional)

Whip cream until stiff. Gradually whip in sugar. Do not over-whip or it will turn to butter. Gently fold in almonds, chocolate and brandy. Grease and line a 9-by-5-by-3 loaf pan or an 8-cup mold with waxed paper. Pour mixture into it. Freeze in ice compartment of refrigerator until stiff. Unmold and cut into thick slices. If desired, serve with a chocolate sauce.

Chocolate Sauce
(CREMA DI CIOCCOLATO)

This sauce is on the thick and bittersweet side. Over hot water, melt 4 ounces (4 squares) semisweet chocolate in 1 cup water. Stir in ¾ tablespoon brandy or more for desired consistency. Serve over spumone.

Easter Pie from the Naples Region
(LA PASTIERA DI GRANA)

An archaic cake with an interesting flavor. The wheat symbolizes fertility, and Easter, time of the Resurrection, stands for new life. Cracked wheat can be bought in Near Eastern and health-food stores.

½ cup cracked wheat
1 quart water
1 cup milk
2 tablespoons butter
¾ cup sugar
2 cups ricotta cheese
Grated rind of 2 lemons
Grated rind of 1 orange

1 tablespoon orange water or brandy
4 eggs, beaten
½ cup pignoli nuts
½ cup raisins, plumped
½ cup minced glacé citron
1 recipe Pasta Frolla
Confectioners' sugar

Soak wheat in water for 10 minutes. Boil for 10 minutes or until soft. Drain. Combine wheat, milk, sugar and butter in large saucepan. Bring to a boil. Cook, stirring frequently, for 10 minutes. Drain off excess liquid. Cream ricotta with lemon and orange peel and brandy until fluffy. Beat in eggs. Add nuts, raisins and citron. Beat in wheat mixture. Roll out Pasta Frolla; reserve one third. Grease and flour a deep 10-inch pie pan. Line bottom and sides with the two thirds of the Pasta Frolla. Pour in filling. Cut remaining Pasta Frolla into strips 1 inch wide. Arrange strips in a lattice pattern over filling. Bake in preheated moderate oven (350° F.) for about 50 to 60 minutes, or until filling is set and crust golden brown. Sprinkle with confectioners' sugar before serving. Makes 12 servings.

Sweet Pastry Dough
(PASTA FROLLA)

This rich dough, one of the standard Italian pastry doughs, requires a bare minimum of handling, or else it will be crumbly.

4 egg yolks
½ cup sugar
2 cups flour
¼ cup butter, creamed

¼ cup lard, creamed
Grated rind of 1 lemon
1 tablespoon brandy

Cream egg yolks with sugar. Beat in ¼ cup of the flour. Cream together butter and lard. Beat into egg mixture. With a fork, stir in remaining flour, lemon rind and brandy. Stir only until the dough is smooth and clears the sides of the bowl in a ball. Shape into a ball. Wrap in waxed paper. Chill for 1 hour or longer before using. Makes 2 8-inch pie shells.

Almond Cake
(TORTA DI MANDORLE)

This plain cake is typical of Italian home baking. Potato starch, also called potato flour, can be bought in Jewish or Scandinavian grocery shops. It is much used for baking in Italy.

3 eggs, separated
⅔ cup sugar
¼ cup potato starch, sifted
½ cup orange juice

1¾ cups ground blanched
almonds
½ teaspoon ground cinnamon

Beat egg yolks and sugar with an electric beater at medium speed for 7 minutes. The mixture should be thick and white. (The original Italian recipe calls for at least 30 minutes of hand beating.) Using beater at low speed, beat in alternately the potato starch and the orange juice. Add almonds and ground cinnamon and mix well. Beat egg whites until stiff and fold into mixture. Grease and flour an 8-inch spring-form pan. Pour in mixture. Bake in preheated slow oven (325° F.) for 35 to 40 minutes or until cake tests clean. This cake is good with a Macedonia, or fruit salad, or with a glass of sweet wine, sherry or Marsala.

Note: Cornstarch may be used instead of potato starch. The cake's texture will be a little less tender, and the cake a little drier.

Sicilian Christmas or Easter Cake

(CASSATA ALLA SICILIANA)

A Cassata may be vanilla ice cream filled with whipped cream, chocolate bits and candied fruit, which is never made at home but eaten in the cafés. Or it can be a cake, as here. There is also a Neapolitan Cassata cake, which consists of a sponge cake filled with custard and garnished with nuts and candied fruit. Ricotta is essential in this recipe, since it gives the Cassata alla Siciliana its typical flavor.

3 cups ricotta cheese
⅓ cup sugar
2 tablespoons milk
3 tablespoons Maraschino liqueur or orange or rose water
1 ounce (1 square) bitter or semisweet chocolate, chopped

¾ cup finely diced mixed candied fruit
1 10-inch sponge cake (homemade or bought)
¼ cup Maraschino (optional)
Frosting
Strips of candied orange peel
Candied cherries

Mix together ricotta, sugar, milk and Maraschino. Force through a strainer and beat until smooth, light and fluffy. Beat in chocolate and candied fruit. Cut the sponge cake into 3 layers. Sprinkle a little Maraschino on each layer. Spread filling between layers—top with cake layer. Chill. Frost just before serving time.

FROSTING

2 to 3 cups sifted confectioners' sugar	2 teaspoons almond flavoring
1 egg white, unbeaten	1 to 2 tablespoons lemon juice

Put 2 cups of the confectioners' sugar, the egg white, almond flavoring and 1 tablespoon of the lemon juice into a bowl. Beat to spreading consistency. If too thin, add a little more confectioners' sugar; if too thick, a little more lemon juice, 1 teaspoon at a time. Reserve ⅓ of the frosting. Frost sides and top of the cake. Beat a drop of red food coloring into remaining frosting. Or divide remaining frosting and color one part red, the other part green. Decorate the Cassata with swirls of colored frosting, strips of orange peel and candied cherries. Makes 8 to 10 servings.

Fruit Bread from Siena

(PANFORTE DI SIENA)

This hard and flavorful fruit cake dates back to the Middle Ages, just like the beautiful city it comes from. It is really excellent and will keep for weeks.

¾ cup blanched almonds
¾ cup filberts, lightly toasted
⅓ cup cocoa
1½ teaspoons cinnamon
¼ teaspoon allspice
½ cup sifted all-purpose flour
¾ cup candied orange peel,
  shredded

¾ cup candied lemon peel,
  shredded
¾ cup candied citron peel,
  shredded
¾ cup honey
¾ cup granulated sugar
Confectioners' sugar mixed
  with cinnamon

Combine all ingredients except honey, granulated sugar and confectioners' sugar. Blend well. Cook honey and granulated sugar over low heat until a little of the syrup dropped into cold water forms a soft ball, or candy thermometer registers 238° F. Stir constantly. Add to fruits and mix thoroughly. Line a buttered 9-inch spring-form pan with well-buttered brown paper. Pour in dough and smooth out with a wet knife blade. Bake in preheated slow (300° F.) oven about 30 minutes. When cool, sprinkle top with confectioners' sugar and cinnamon.

All Souls' Day Macaroons

(FAVE DEI MORTI)

From Southern Italy, where special foods are prepared for November 2, All Souls' Day, to commemorate the dead.

1 cup unblanched almonds
1⅓ cups sugar
1 teaspoon ground cinnamon
1 cup sifted all-purpose flour

2 tablespoons butter
Grated rind of 2 lemons
2 eggs, beaten

Grind almonds very fine in nut grinder or electric blender. Combine almonds, sugar and cinnamon. Sift together through a strainer into a deep bowl. Add flour, butter, lemon rind and eggs. Mix with a spoon until mixture clings together. With hands, knead into a smooth paste or until mixture no longer clings to hands. Shape into 1-inch loaves and flatten top of leaves. Grease and flour 2 cooky sheets. Put macaroons on them, leaving at least a 1-inch space between cookies. Bake in preheated moderate oven (350° F.) for 15 to 20 minutes, or until edges are golden brown. Let cool on sheets for 5 minutes. Makes about 70 macaroons.

Index